POV Press
Books by Bethanne Kim

SURVIVAL SKILLS FOR ALL AGES #2

26 Mental & Urban Life Skills

BETHANNE KIM

Cover photo from the Carol M. Highsmith Collection at the Library of Congress, image #04178.

1. Non-fiction-Family & Relationships-Reference
2. Education & Reference-Reference-Survival & Emergency Preparedness

Paperback ISBN: 978-1-942533-29-0
Ebook ISBN: 978-1-942533-30-6

Distributed by POV Press LLC
PO Box 399
Catharpin, VA 20143

Printed in the United States of America

Dedication

For all the Scout leaders who helped ingrain "Be Prepared" into me
at the very deepest levels of who I am.

And for the young Scouts, including my sons, that I am encouraging
to Be Prepared in their own lives.

Table of Contents

{PART 1}
EMOTIONAL WELL-BEING

I f we curl up in a corner and won't do anything, it doesn't really matter what knowledge or skills we have because we aren't using them. It doesn't matter if we are depressed or terrified or lonely or whatever, we have been thoroughly sidelined from life.

Have Faith: Faith gives us strength to persevere even when things look hopeless. Faith helps us believe things will improve, no matter how bad they look or feel in the moment.

Set Goals: Goals help us get where we are going. Without goals, we are just adrift in a sea of (hopefully good) intentions.

Hard Emotions: Anger, fear, jealousy, boredom, heartbreak—there are many emotions that can make it hard to accomplish anything. Mastering these emotions is a huge step toward reaching your goals.

Be Calm and Handle Stress: Panicking never helps get anything done. Staying calm and making plans gets us moving forward, toward our goals, and helps us handle stress. This seems to be a bigger problem all the time in our world. Handling stress well is a big advantage in life, no matter what you do.

Pressure: Pressure can come from peers, family, and or yourself. But pressure can be positive as well as negative. Positive pressure helps us do things that help us improve ourselves. Like stress, dealing with pressure is one of our biggest challenges.

{ONE}

HAVE FAITH

In times of crisis, almost everyone, no matter their age or how much power they have, feel the need to pray. The most common prayers go to the God of Moses and Abraham, because the Jewish God is ultimately also the God of Christians and Muslims as well. It seems like that makes Him the God of more people than any other on Earth. That does not make Him the only God people pray to. There are many faiths, with many Gods and Goddesses or none at all. Some simply pray to whatever force is out there.

> **Personal note:** I refer to God as He for one simple reason: My then-toddler son told me God is a man, like him. He remembered sensing His presence when he nearly died as an infant.

Whoever or whatever you pray to, a strong faith in something greater than yourself is good for your mental and physical health. It is good for surviving, full stop, disaster or no disaster. **Faith gives us the strength we need when life gets difficult,** even if that difficulty is "only" struggling with a class or classmate at school.

Having faith doesn't mean that you will be "rewarded" by having things happen just as you hope, when you just hope. Having faith means believing that things will work out for the best, eventually.

Sometimes it doesn't feel like it's working out for the best, especially if it's painful, but that doesn't mean it isn't really for the best.

Jim Collins wrote the book *Good to Great*. In it, he discusses something he called the "Stockdale Paradox." There is an article with a longer description of it in the Resources section of this chapter but the basic idea is that optimists don't always fare the best in truly dire circumstances. When things don't work out, they can lose heart and hope. They expect to get to their goal fairly easily without a lot of road blocks slowing them down. Realists fare best. They are fully aware of how bad their situation is and work to improve their present situation to help reach their goal. Set-backs and frustrations have less of an effect because they expect them, making pushing through them easier. They have faith that they will get to their goal *eventually,* not necessarily *immediately.*

Faith helps people stay strong even in the worst circumstances but you have to believe that God, the Universe, or whatever you call it knows best. If you set tests–"If you love me, I will get an A on this test"–then you are demanding God follow your rules and expectations and that's not how it works. He sees and knows more than you can.

One of my sons was struggling with some problems at school and had been for a long time. One night, I prayed with all my heart for God to guide me in helping my son. **I didn't ask for a specific path. I asked for guidance and help.** The next day, he made some comments at school–*less than twelve hours later*–that resulted in me being called in and forced to get him some fairly specific help *immediately*, that same day. Up until then, I had considered that path but avoided it because I thought it was too much. It was exactly right. I had prayed for help before but it wasn't until I was open to whatever God felt best that I was truly able to help him, and it did help him.

When we ask for something specific, God may not listen because He knows it isn't what we need. When we are open to letting Him set the course and the timing, then we truly have faith and He can help us.

Ask God for help and guidance. Trust that He will lead you where you *need* to be, even if it isn't where you *want* to be

Morals

Strong faith provides many things but one of the most important is the foundation for a moral life. That's a fancy way of saying **it helps you to know, in your heart and your mind, the difference between right and wrong and to want to do right, not wrong.**

Pray–and Listen to the Answers!

Just, pray. Ask for help. Ask for guidance. Pour out your troubles. Tell God in great detail what you want and think you need. As much as I think generally simply asking for help and guidance is the quickest route to getting it, being specific sometimes isn't a bad thing. Maybe what you are hoping for is close to what God is planning anyhow!

But when you pray, remember to ***listen to the answers***. A lot of times, they come through as a whisper. I went on a cruise, leaving my family at home. It was hard for me to do but I kept feeling like I was meant to go alone. While I was on the cruise, I actually overcame a long-time fear of water. I probably would not have confronted and overcame this fear if they had been with me. I definitely would not have if I had stayed home the way my bank account encouraged me to do. (To be clear: I saved money and spent very little to make sure I didn't create a financial problem for my family.)

When I was given the chance to go, I didn't expect that outcome. I wanted my husband to come with me. (Our kids couldn't skip school.) But I had this recurring feeling that I should go alone, even though I didn't know why. It wasn't until the fear hit me and I started working through it that I understood. But I had faith that there was a reason I had to go and I had to go alone.

You may not understand, or even like, the answers you receive but pay attention. Talk to your parents or youth pastor if you need more guidance.

Read and Memorize Verses

Read. Your parents and teachers are right–reading is fundamental. Read the Holy Book for your faith whether it is the Bible (Christian), the Torah (Jewish), the Qur'an (Muslim), the Dhammapada (Buddhist), the Bhagavad Gita (Hindu), or something else entirely. For that matter, read more than one. Reading the Holy Book of another faith may make you think more about your own faith or think about it in a different way.

> *"He abused me, he beat me, he defeated me, he robbed me,"--in those who harbor such thoughts hatred will never cease.*

That is from the Dhammapada, a book of Buddha's teachings, but those of other faiths can appreciate the principles. Many of the basic concepts of love and forgiveness are the same across faiths. Reading a new book in your own faith can have the same effect.

Now try memorizing some verses from what you have read. Rote memorization (memorizing words exactly as written with no regard to understanding or analyzing them) isn't done very much anymore but it definitely has a place in life. The main time I see anyone doing this is when they, occasionally, need to memorize a long list of instructions or directions. Memorizing verses from your faith is a good way to practice rote memorization.

Memorizing verses is also good because **no one can ever take away what is in your head**. If there is an emergency, any verses you memorized are still there, in your head. You can recite them to yourself or others for comfort. If there are any you do not understand, you can think on them or discuss them as a distraction.

Sing

My Mom always says that singing is an outward sign of an inward joy. In my case, it sounds out more like an outward sign of inward dying animal, but that doesn't make her wrong. I love to sing! Singing is a wonderful way to show your faith, joy, and happiness. It also helps work through sorrow, anger, and pain.

Singing can be relaxing, energizing, calming, reassuring, empowering.... It really depends on what you choose and how it makes you feel. Music I play when I am in a bad mood is music some of my friends play when they are particularly cheerful.

Play around, listen to lots of different kinds, and see what tickles your fancy. Let iTunes create some new Genius playlists for you. Go to an online radio site or app and listen to at least five stations with music you never normally listen to, including at least one classical station. There is a reason this music is still popular after hundreds of years.

Activity

Memorize two verses from your faith's Holy Book.

OR

Create a few playlists of music that makes you feel different ways. Include one that helps you feel calmer when you are stressed, afraid, or angry. If you don't have an electronic device to make one on, ask your parents if you can make one on their device. Odds are good that you can find at least a few of their songs that you like, if they aren't willing to import any of yours. If all else fails, just write a list of music that you would make into a playlist if you could.

Quick Quiz

T/F   Music can help you feel calmer and more relaxed.

T/F   Strong morals help you know right from wrong.

T/F　　It's important to listen for the answer when you pray.

T/F　　Memorizing religious verses has no benefit to you.

T/F　　Strong faith does not help in dangerous situations.

Resources

Articles

Documentary Traces Faith of POWs
assets.baptiststandard.com/archived/2000/6_5/pages/pows.html

The Stockdale Paradox
www.ndoherty.com/stockdale-paradox/

Books

How to Memorize the Bible Fast and Easy by Adam Houge

Moonwalking with Einstein: The Art and Science of Remembering Everything by Joshua Foer

NIV Bible for Teens

Wide Awake: A Buddhist Guide for Teens by Diana Winston

Other

Verse Rain: Bible Verse Memorization Game (App)

Scouting-Specific

Pray Publishing (religious awards for all ages and dozens of faiths)
www.praypub.org/main_frameset.htm

{TWO}

SET GOALS

Everyone, no matter their age, has goals–things they haven't done yet but want to do. As we get older, our goals become more complex and longer term. They advance from grabbing our toes to walking to making people understand us to school and sports goals to eventually getting into college and getting a good job, then seeing our children, grandchildren, and even great-grandchildren do the same things.

What do you really want to do but can't? This might be related to Part 2: Financial Savvy if it requires earning and saving money to buy something your parents can't afford to buy, or won't pay for (assuming they approve of you having it). It might be earning permission to have or do something. It could be earning better grades. It could even be what you want to be when you grow up (even if you are already "grown up"). Most of us have many goals at a time but only a few we are really working toward and even fewer that really matter. Think about the goals you have that you care about achieving the most. Focus on those and let the others wait.

Whatever it is, a goal should be something specific you really, truly want, not just a passing wish. A lot of people choose "lose weight," "eat healthy," and "exercise" as New Year's Resolutions (goals). These are *terrible* goals because they are so generic. "Lose 5 pounds by

March," "eat one serving of vegetables a day for three weeks," and "exercise for ten minutes every day for a month" are all specific, measurable, reachable goals. **Specific, Measurable, Achievable, Relevant, and Time-bound (SMART) goals are good goals.**

You can have very generic goals like "exercise more" in your head. You can also have very large goals that take a long time to reach, like "walk on the moon," in your head. There is nothing wrong with that! Sometimes thinking about generic goals gets you moving in the right direction. And it's great to have HUGE goals! You'll never get there without goals–but to actually get the whole way there, those big goals need broken down into smaller, easier steps and the SMART acronym is very commonly used to help people with goal-setting.

Write Down Your Goals

Write down your top goals. Put them in order and note if they are for personal, school, family/home, sports, faith, etc. Here are some examples:

- **Personal:** I will write a 100 word poem and submit it to at least three magazines within one month.
- **School:** I will improve my math grade to a B+ and stop getting "needs improvement" for my handwriting during the next marking period.
- **Family:** I will bring my dirty laundry to the laundry room every Friday after school and put away my clean laundry as soon as Mom leaves it in my room.
- **Sports:** I will do all the stretches and other exercises coach assigns me to do at home every night for at least one month.
- **Faith:** I will pray before I go to bed every night, even when I am super tired.

If you re-read those, every one of them starts with "I will", not "I might" or "I'll try to". It is a promise to yourself that you *will* do what you are setting out to achieve. Each goal is SMART.

Breaking it Down

Sometimes the experiences along the journey are the reason for it. On a road trip, stopping and seeing whatever strikes your fancy may be the main purpose. **This is the exact opposite of goal setting.** (OK, technically it isn't if the goal is to have no goal beyond the trip itself and experiencing new things but I think you understand the point.)

If you do not know where you are going, you will never get there. Period. The first step is writing the steps you need to complete to reach your goal. They should be specific, clear, reachable, and measurable, just like the goal itself. They should also be *possible*. Some goals, like walking on the moon, are so large or complicated that they have to be broken down into many (many) smaller goals. "Become an astronaut" is one step of that but is that something you can just do or is that more of a sub-goal?

When you find a sub-goal, you need to write the steps to reach that. For something as big as "walk on the moon," there will be many sub-goals, including attending a top college, getting good grades, and not getting into trouble with the law. (A criminal record effectively makes many dreams and goals impossible.)

Defining Success

If you have a clear, specific goal, then success is probably defined within it. If not, then go back and work on making it clearer and more specific. Either way, remember to be flexible. Life changes. If we end up landing on Mars, your goal might change to "be in the first group of Mars settlers." Or you might realize that you hate–truly *hate*–isolation of any kind, making space travel less appealing. So perhaps working on designing space vehicles or studying objects brought back from the moon (or Mars) will be a better fit.

There is not a thing wrong with updating your goals when circumstances or information change.

Understand Your Reasons

Be clear with yourself on why you want to reach this goal. Your reasons can affect how well you stay on track and how you work toward your goal. It is much easier to stay on track when you are doing things because you love them or are extremely interested in them than if you are doing it to make someone else happy. No matter how old you are, that never changes. The other thing that never changes is the need to do things to make the ones you love or who have power over you (like bosses and teachers) happy.

Here is an example: There are many reasons to want to be an Eagle Scout/earn your Gold Award. If someone works toward these because they love Scouting, they are very internally motivated and it won't take as much to stay on track because it is *fun* for them. If it is to help get jobs throughout life, that is another entirely internal reason but it might be harder to stay motivated if they decide it doesn't make much of a difference. Internal motivation is very powerful.

If they are working on their Gold/Eagle is to please their parents or grandparents or to impress someone else, it will be much harder to stay on track because it isn't a goal they really, truly care about in their heart. It is something to make other people happy, not the goal-setter. That doesn't mean they won't achieve their goal, simply that it will be easier for them to get distracted and off-track.

Understanding your reasons also makes it easier to set a deadline for achieving your goal. If you want to gain or lose weight to make a sports team, then the date tryouts start is your deadline. If you want to lose weight to feel better about how you look, then you don't have such a clear deadline.

Being Responsible

It is quite simple really. **Whether or not you reach any goal you set is on *you*, not your parents, your teachers, your siblings, or anyone else.**

But they didn't…. They could've…. Why didn't they…. You wail. Well, why didn't YOU? If it was something you can't do (drive somewhere before you are 16, for example), was there another way you could've done it? Is there another person who would've driven you? Mass transit (a bus or train) that could've taken you? Uber?

Staying Motivated

Remaining motivated and helping those around us–at home, in clubs, and later at work–succeed while we work toward our goals are important. Without motivation, we simply stall and stop making progress toward our goals. Being self-motivated means doing things we are supposed to, such as chores and homework, without being reminded all the time. Like so many things, all of this is far more easily said than done but it *can* be done.

It is only human to have trouble remaining motivated. Having a friend or partner is one way to remain motivated. You can check in on each other to make sure you are meeting goals and sub-goals. Sometimes just knowing you will have to tell someone else if you mess up is enough to stay motivated. At the same time, many goals require help from others. If we do not work well with others and help them when they need it, then they will be unwilling to help us meet our goals.

When we set goals, we have to work to achieve them and that forces us to act and to be accountable for our actions. If we do not complete a task, then we do not get closer to our goals. If you don't already have a list of reasons you want to reach your goal, go back and create one. Refer to it as needed. You can even post it somewhere you will see it all the time, including as the wallpaper when you open your tablet/phone/other device.

If the problem is that you are having zero fun, rethink what you are doing and how you are doing it. Ask someone you trust, like your parents or a teacher, for help. There should be a way to make it more fun for you. Life shouldn't be miserable! Know in advance, though, that the answer may be a change in your attitude and how you are looking at the task. It may even be "suck it up, buttercup" because sometimes we all do have to suck it up, buttercup.

Sometimes, the problem is pressure from others. If your teacher, project partner, friend, parent, or anyone else is, with the best of intentions, making it hard for you to stay motivated, try talking to them. Let them know what you have done recently and what you plan to do next, and when you plan to do it. They may have good feedback to help you move forward. Knowing that you have a plan and are still hard at work, assuming you are, usually makes other people (like parents) feel less stressed about your ability to reach a goal, and that leads to them pressuring you less. If you aren't actually all that hard at work, talking to them and talking through any obstacles you are facing is a good way to re-motivate yourself and get going again.

When you are working toward a big goal, it's OK to give yourself little rewards along the way. That doesn't mean asking for a big (or even little) present. It might mean asking to go hang out with a friend for a few hours during a time you could be working. It might be taking a break to go swing in a hammock in the yard. It might be baking brownies and eating them fresh from the oven. Whatever it is, small rewards when you finish a chunk of a big project can be great for staying motivated.

Working with Others

Small goals can be accomplished without help. Putting away one basket of folded laundry? Yeah, you got that. Washing, drying,

34

sorting, folding, and putting away six loads of laundry? Hey, wasn't that a squirrel outside?!? Let's go look.....

Yep, you saw what I did there and so would anyone else working with me. I got distracted and stopped working. Having a partner or friend there makes it harder for literal or figurative squirrels to derail your progress. Of course, there is always the chance that the other person will, themselves, become a distraction, so be careful to stay on track.

Activity

Set a goal that requires at least a few days of work, and work toward it. Break it down so you work on it a little bit each day. When you finish, give yourself a reward!

Quick Quiz

T/F   Working with others to reach a goal is always a mistake

T/F   Breaking down your goal into manageable steps is an important part of reaching your goals.

T/F   Staying motivated can be tough, even for adults.

T/F   You should find someone else to blame when you don't reach a goal.

T/F   Knowing why you want to reach a goal is never important.

Resources

Articles

11 Effective Goal Setting Templates for You
stunningmotivation.com/11-effective-goal-setting-templates-for-you/

5 Reasons You Should Set Big Goals
www.lifehack.org/articles/productivity/the-5-reasons-you-should-set-big-goals.html

Forget About Setting Goals. Focus on This Instead.
jamesclear.com/goals-systems

Golden Rules of Goal Setting
www.mindtools.com/pages/article/newHTE_90.htm

How to Stay Motivated
www.lifehack.org/articles/productivity/how-to-stay-motivated.html

How to Set Goals
www.wikihow.com/Set-Goals

The Science of Breaking Out of Your Comfort Zone (and Why You Should)
lifehacker.com/the-science-of-breaking-out-of-your-comfort-zone-and-w-656426705

Setting Smart Goals (includes a worksheet and template)
www.smartsheet.com/blog/essential-guide-writing-smart-goals

Smart Goal Setting for Teens
7mindsets.com/smart-goal-setting-for-teens/

Books

Goal Setting (Workbook Included): Goals & Motivation: Introduction To A Complete & Proven Step-By-Step Blueprint For Reaching Your Goals by Martin Kaye

Goal Setting Journal: The Best Goal Setting Tool by Elizabeth Earl (Note: Buy the paperback, not the Kindle version, per the author.)

S.M.A.R.T. Goals Made Simple: 10 Steps to Master Your Personal and Career Goals by S.J. Scott

Other

3 Goal Setting Templates (pdf)
www.mytimemanagement.com/goal-setting-templates.html

Goals: Setting and Achieving Them on Schedule by Zig Ziglar (audio CD or audible)

SMART Goals for Teens (pdf)
www.tlplearningsolutions.com/docs/SMART_Goals_Teens_2011.pdf

Scouting-Specific

Independence Badge
forgirls.girlscouts.org/home/badgeexplorer/#independence

Videos

Questions Every Teenager Needs to Be Asked | Laurence Lewars | TEDxDhahranHighSchool
www.youtube.com/watch?v=NEgoEgonx3U

Michael Hyatt Podcast: Goal Setting for Beginners [Season 4 Ep 8]
michaelhyatt.com/season-4-episode-08-goal-setting-for-beginners-podcast.html

{THREE}

HARD EMOTIONS

I debated what to call this chapter because calling certain emotions "negative" might make is sound like they are bad and should be avoided but that's impossible to do. We all have bad days. Even on good days, we can have feelings that are uncomfortable, bad, negative, or whatever you call them. These emotions can be tough to handle but they don't have to be. It's important to remember that they are normal and it's OK to experience them. Problems start when they just keep hanging on instead of being "processed" so you can move back to being happier.

No matter what the emotion is, the basic process is the same. Deal with the emotion in a way that doesn't cause problems for other people. Think about whether this is really a problem or just something you don't like or didn't expect. Talk to your closest, most trusted friends and family to work through it and learn from the experience but remember that your very closest loved ones aren't always the best choice. Sometimes they get angry/hurt/whatever on our behalf if we tell them all the gory details of what happened so you may need a close friend instead of a best friend or parent. Repeat if necessary, then go on with your life.

Actually going through all those steps can take anywhere from minutes to a lifetime, depending on how serious the issue is. The important thing to remember is that you don't have to do it all alone. Your friends and loved ones generally want to help you, as long as you don't get too needy for too long. They also need you to articulate what you need from them, don't expect them to be mind-readers. Needing someone to listen or to offer possible solutions are two very different needs. Try to pick someone who is temperamentally suited to what you need. Most of us have some friends and some family who are naturally more introverted, and thus more likely to listen, and others who love to offer solutions to any problem that comes up. If you go to the person naturally inclined to do what you need, it will be easier and happier for everyone.

The biggest problem with some of these emotions is that many of us dwell on our problems, thinking about them endlessly, going over them again and again in our minds. After a certain point, this goes from being helpful (figuring out what went wrong and how to do better next time) to making things worse. Dwelling on a problem can intensify emotions as well as making them hang around longer, neither of which is good for you. For all of the emotions in this section, if you have been thinking about nothing but the source of your negative emotion for more than a day, there is a good chance you are starting to dwell. Try to distract yourself so you start to feel better and can work toward improving your situation, if necessary.

Anger (Frustration)

Even the Dalia Lama gets angry and he is a very high level Buddhist, a faith renowned for the peacefulness of its practitioners. Anger is human and it can be good. If more Americans had been angry when Japanese civilians were interned in WWII, perhaps we could have avoided that chapter in our history. The anger of a single mother in 1980 led her to create MADD: Mothers Against Drunk Driving. MADD successfully fought to decrease drunk driving. **Anger can be good IF it causes you to fight against injustice or danger.**

What about other times? The first step is to take some slow, calming breaths. Imagine breathing in calm and breathing out anger. When you are a bit calmer, ask yourself how big a deal the problem really is. Often, the things that make us angry aren't that big a deal. In fact, in my personal experience, an awful lot is really just frustration. Stop to take a break and do something else when you start getting frustrated and *before you get to the point of being angry*. Come back when you feel less frustrated. Just doing this will probably decrease how often you get angry.

Sometimes we get angry because things aren't the way we expected or wanted them to be. That doesn't actually mean they are bad, just different. If this is why you are mad, stop and think about whether it is really worse or just different. It might even be better, once you think about it. One of my sons used to get mad at me every single time I moved his things (primarily furniture). It was *change* and he hates change. Over time, he has learned that change isn't always bad, like the day his brother moved out. Now he has his own room. He still isn't happy with change but he doesn't get angry about it now.

There might be a good reason for things being different. Just ask.

Anxiety (Worry)

Anxiety can be a debilitating problem that requires medication and the help of a mental health professional but it doesn't reach that level for most people. When anxiety is caused by chemical imbalances, doctor-prescribed medication helps. If you have so much anxiety that it is interfering with your daily life, see your primary care doctor for help. This is no more "your fault" than having crooked teeth and should be judged about the same as getting braces.

It isn't uncommon for insecurity to mask itself as anxiety. We don't feel smart enough, skilled enough, attractive enough,_____ enough. We don't feel like we did a good enough job. Anxiety can be caused by stressful life events: scary medical diagnoses, losing or starting a job, starting or ending a relationship (dating, marriage, long-term friendship, even family relationships), and moving are just a few of them.

Like so many things, it sounds overly simplistic, but focusing on other things really can do wonders. Once you've distracted yourself a bit, think about what you can do to be less anxious. Practicing a skill is a great way to feel less anxious about how you will do, and that most definitely includes schoolwork. If it's something you can't change like how smart you, look around yourself. There is almost certainly something you are better at than most people. There is almost certainly someone who isn't as smart as you. Even the smartest people are never "the smartest" about everything. The lead characters on the TV show *The Big Bang Theory* are extremely smart men and women but none of them knows everything about everything. If a fictional character like Sheldon Cooper isn't always the smartest one in the room, how on earth could a real human being hope to be?

If you are anxious about your looks, the same thing is true. "Beauty" is a fairly subjective thing. Beauty, in our modern culture, is also relatively easy to improve. Make-up, hairstyles, clothing, even surgery are all available–for a price. To be clear, I am not advocating surgery but there are times when it is a legitimate choice, particularly if an accident has led to scarring or disfigurement. It may also be a good choice if it is correcting a physical problem such as back pain or breathing difficulties. If you are contemplating surgery for your looks and it isn't to correct scarring, disfigurement, or a physical problem, are you sure that you need it? Why?

The best remedy for anxiety has been demonstrated, repeatedly, to be exercise. In addition to lowering your stress levels, your body will become more fit and toned. If your body (appearance or health) are a source of anxiety, this makes exercising doubly beneficial.

Boredom

Find something to do. Anything. Dust. Research something online. Go for a bike ride. Reorganize your room. Just DO something. If you don't, there is a very good chance your parents (boss, roommate, etc.) will find something for you to do. If you think dusting sounds boring, an over-worked mom/boss faced with a person complaining of boredom can come up with something far worse. Do not test this. Whatever you do, it should be mentally challenging and/or keep you moving.

Depression

This is really just an extreme version of sadness. You can be depressed for as little as a few minutes or for decades. If you are depressed enough that it is affecting your ability to live—schoolwork, friends, work—then you need to talk to your parents or another adult such as a teacher, church youth leader, boss, or counselor to help you find professional help. If they don't listen, keep searching until you find an adult who does help. It may be the hardest thing you ever do, but getting help is worth the discomfort and stress.

There is no shame in depression or getting treatment for depression, including medication and talk therapy. It is important to get professional treatment promptly for depression that lasts more than a few weeks. If you don't treat it, depression can last for years but treatment can help you enjoy life again.

Disappointment

Whether it's a present, admission to an elite group, or doing something you've been looking forward to, we all have times we don't get what we wanted, or expected. We're disappointed. Once the initial emotions subside, take time to think about what you could have done differently to have more success. Talk to your boss, parents, coach, or teachers for their perspective, and really listen to what they have to say—especially if you don't like it. They want you to succeed, so they will give you their best advice to help make that happen.

Envy

Envy is when you want to have something that belongs to another person. The basic problem with envy is that if you focus on what others have, there will always be something you want. Always. You need to focus on what it is that you have in your own life and how it makes you happy. If it doesn't, then focus on how to make your own life better. Taking something from someone else won't make your life better.

Obviously, this is far, far, far easier said than done (and often subconscious), so just take it one step at a time. First of all, recognize that there are more than two choices. If you are envious someone won the lead in a play, you might be the understudy and perform some nights. You might also find another aspect you enjoy such as House Manager or Prop Master. You might also work on your skills so you win the next lead. There is almost certainly another choice that will make fit your needs well enough. Whenever you start to think envious thoughts, make a conscious choice to think about something else. It may be something totally different to distract yourself or you may choose to focus on a way to improve your own life so you are content with it. As simplistic as it sounds, this really is the easiest way to handle envy.

Fear

It feels as safe as entering a burning building filled with dynamite. You want to run as far and fast as you can, or maybe you want to run to the closest person you love and trust so they can hold and protect and avoid it. Taking even a single step toward doing it is impossibly difficult. **"It" is something different for every person. "It" is your biggest fear. Compared to that, everything else is manageable.**

HARD EMOTIONS

There are things we should be afraid of and avoid at all costs, like an actual burning building full of dynamite or people trying to force us to do things we know are wrong. Most things we are afraid of really won't hurt us. The stress our fear creates causes more problems than actually being in a small space, heights, spiders, public speaking (even by our parents), shots, or any other common fear ever will. Let your parents and loved ones help. They know you and probably have some good suggestions, even if they sound not-so-helpful to you. The biggest thing you can do to get over your fear is simply to do it but it's OK to start with baby steps. The following example is public speaking, but the same principals apply to just about any fear: start small, get bigger, and learn more about what scares you.

You may start with a big goal like giving a speech in front of your entire grade but you start with much smaller sub-goals. First step, write the speech. Second step, practice in front of a mirror, alone–or even just plain alone, no mirror. Next, practice in front of your parents and grandparents. Keep adding more people as you become more comfortable. You may be able to take a public speaking class at your school or a local college, or join (or start) a Toastmasters Junior group. If you take a class or join Toastmasters, you will receive a lot of feedback to become a better speaker and the practice should help you be less afraid. Toastmasters is popular for just this reason.

With a fear like spiders or snakes, learning facts may help. If you are afraid to go swimming with friends because there may be snakes in the pond or a spider might hide in your shoe, fear is keeping you from fully enjoying your life. Knowing what kinds of snakes live near you (there may not even be any poisonous snakes) and recognizing that you can shake out your shoes and clothing to remove spiders can go far toward easing your fears. Many fears are like that: a little knowledge can work miracles.

Some fears have solid evolutionary reasons but they don't need to be paralyzing. It's OK to remain a bit afraid. You don't need a pet snake to consider your fear reasonably conquered, you just need to reach the point it doesn't interfere with your life.

Heartbreak

When people talk about having a broken heart, they usually mean a romantic relationship ending, but that isn't the only kind of heart break. Finding out that a "best friend" is anything but, being forced to stop a much-loved activity, really anything that makes you lose something or someone you love can lead to heartbreak.

Spending time with people you love who love you back, like your parents, grandparents, close friends, and possibly siblings or cousins, is a great way to start letting your heart heal. You will probably also need some time alone. And, male or female, some tears will fall if your heart was really broken. And that's OK, because they will stop. Letting them flow for a bit gets them out so they are gone and you can move on with healing.

This is one case where the remedy really is waiting for time to heal your wounds. Eventually, it will.

Jealousy

Jealousy is when you are afraid someone is going to take something of yours, generally something that you care deeply about or even love. Unlike most of the other emotions discussed in this chapter, jealous isn't a solitary emotion. You can't be jealous without another person's involvement. The most important step toward conquering jealousy is simply recognizing and truly accepting that people, and animals, can love more than one person. Loving a new person doesn't make the others any less loved.

Do you love your mom? And your dad? And your grandparents? Do your parents love each other and you and your grandparents and any other children they have? Do your grandparents love each other and you and your parents and all their other children and grandchildren?

Jealousy is just a fear that you haven't conquered. No one can take away another person's love for you or their friendship. *No one.*

Activity

Conquer a fear, or at least take baby steps to start taming it.

Quick Quiz

T/F   Anger can be good.

T/F   When you need help, it may take a few tries to find the right person.

T/F   Fears often make things seem worse than they really seem.

T/F   Anxiety is never a big deal, certainly not enough to interfere with daily life.

T/F   When you are upset, spending time with loved ones can help.

Resources

Articles

10 Questions for the Dalai Lama (Time Magazine)
www.dalailama.com/messages/transcripts/10-questions-time-magazine

Depression: What You Need to Know
www.nimh.nih.gov/health/publications/depression-what-you-need-to-know-12-2015/index.shtml

Envy as a Major Source of Anxiety and Discontent
www.psychologytoday.com/us/blog/envy/201205/envy-major-source-anxiety-and-discontent

Five Ways to Kick the Jealousy Habit
www.psychologytoday.com/us/blog/romance-redux/201104/five-ways-kick-the-jealousy-habit

How to Conquer Jealousy
www.yogaofsrichinmoy.com/the-earth-plane/life-problems/jealousy/

Kristen Bell Pens Honest Essay Reminding us There's Nothing Shameful about Depression
www.scarymommy.com/kristen-bell-writes-motto-essay-depression

Melting Envy: The Brilliance of Understanding and Gratitude
www.psychologytoday.com/us/blog/envy/201312/melting-envy-the-brilliance-understanding-and-gratitude

Books

The Anger Workbook by Lee Carter, PhD and Frank Minirth, MD

Conquer Negative Thinking for Teens: A Workbook to Break the Nine Thought Habits that are Holding You Back by Mary Karapatian Alvord, PhD

Happiness Boot Camp: Positive Changes to Get Happy in7 Days by H. Granville James

Hope over Anxiety: How to smash crippling anxiety and live the life you will love! by Christopher Moss

How to Fight and *Anger: Wisdom for Cooling the Flames* by Thich Nhat Hanh

How to Get Unstuck from the Negative Muck by Lake Sullivan, PhD

Retrain Your Brain: Cognitive Behavioral Therapy in 7 Weeks: A Workbook for Managing Depression and Anxiety by Seth J. Gillihan, PhD

Stuff That Sucks: A Teen's Guide to Accepting What You Can't Change and Committing to What You Can by Ben Sedley

Upward Spiral: Using Neuroscience to Reverse the Course of Depression One Small Change at a Time by Alex Korb, PhD

Scouting-Specific

Animal Helpers Badge
forgirls.girlscouts.org/home/badgeexplorer/#animal-helpers

Science of Happiness Badge
forgirls.girlscouts.org/home/badgeexplorer/#science-of-happiness

Videos

10 Minute Guided Meditation to ease Anxiety, Worry, and Urgency
www.youtube.com/watch?v=xoYnqvadurg

How being heartbroken was the best thing to ever happen to me:
Emma Gibbs at TEDxSouthBankWomen
www.youtube.com/watch?v=jCiBQu1TAgY

How to Overcome Fear: Alex Weber Shows You 5 Ways to Break
Free from Fear | Goalcast
www.youtube.com/watch?v=APrR4FhBpI0

Reprogramming your brain to overcome fear: Olympia LePoint at
TEDxPCC
www.youtube.com/watch?v=1PV7Hy_8fhA

Tony Robbins: How To Understand And Conquer Your Fears (
Tony Robbins Motivation)
www.youtube.com/watch?v=aBOMaKVfcMI

Why you're trying to beat boredom the wrong way
www.youtube.com/watch?v=yJeBZECoir0

{FOUR}

BE CALM AND HANDLE STRESS

I n emergencies, panic kills. Panicked people do stupid things, and they make stupid mistakes. Panic, worry, and stress make even the most careful person miss important information and make situational awareness virtually impossible.

Even without an emergency, stress and panic kill…eventually. It's just bad for your body. If you Google "stress symptoms" or "stress health", you will find a ton of information on just how and why stress is bad for your body in the short and long term. Learning to remain truly calm is great for your health and well-being, and it's a skill not a lot of people have.

No matter how old or young we are, we all need to be responsible for our own actions *and reactions* in life. If your brother hits you in the head and you trip him in response, he will almost certainly yell and your parents will punish you, and possibly him. Being responsible for your own *actions* means that he needs to acknowledge that hitting you caused you to trip him. Being responsible for your own *reactions* means you need to accept that you wouldn't have gotten in trouble if you had yelled for help instead of trying to "punish" (or "parent") him yourself. (That's not your job.)

Learning to be responsible for your own actions and reactions will, believe it or not, help you remain calm. When you stop wasting time making excuses and trying to blame others, it is a lot faster and easier to get back to a normal place when something goes wrong. (Part of that is because you aren't making everyone around you more upset by blaming others and making excuses.) If this bugs you because some things are completely beyond your control, you'll get no argument from me. School schedules and requirements, job options, transportation, and a host of other things are based on choices other people make that you can't influence as a teenager. (For adults who don't get this, check out the video "5 Reasons Teens are More Stressed than Adults" in the Resources section.) Some of this changes when you are an adult (it's easier to move to a new city, for example) but not all of it. I would *love* to drive a Duesenberg, for example, but since they make a Rolls Royce look affordable, that's not gonna happen.

It's important to accept that no one has 100% control of their life. Barack Obama was reportedly thrilled when he left office and was allowed to surf and do other water sports deemed "too dangerous" while he was President. Secret Service restricted his activities to keep him safe. The first six people in line for the English throne aren't allowed to get married without permission from the monarch. None of us (including royalty, heads of state, parents, teachers, and bosses) are free to do anything we please.

Most of this chapter is on ways to handle stress. Meditating is probably the easiest and is free, as are calm breathing and physical activity. Really, the most effective stress reducers are all free and easy. You just need to do them. No one else even needs to know what you are doing. Some were already discussed in the Chapter Three.

What is Stress?

So, what is stress and how is it bad? Stress is related to the "fight or flight" response. When our body stays in this state for too long (stress), we start to get sick. Headaches and stomachaches are common problems related to high stress. Kids have stress over schoolwork, friends, family fights, even money. If your coach, teacher, club advisor, or someone else is pressuring you to work harder and it's stressing you out, talk to an adult you trust, hopefully one of your parents. They may be able to find a way for you to lower your stress, even if it means changing your schedule and cutting back on the total number of activities to focus on doing one or two well instead of four or five so-so.

They may also agree that too much is being asked and help you talk to the group leader to improve the situation. If it is a situation that really won't improve, they may take you out of it. If you are in a sport or club and another person does something that makes you uncomfortable or stresses you out and they tell you that you'll get in trouble for talking about what they are doing, think about it for a minute. How is it your fault? It isn't. If they are desperate for you to not talk about what they are doing, it's almost a guarantee that they know it is wrong and quite possibly criminal. By telling your parents or another adult you trust if they don't listen, you have a shot at stopping them from hurting anyone else.

Parents aren't mind readers and, honestly, they've heard you complaining about things since before you could talk. If you are fussing that a teacher "isn't nice" or "doesn't like" you, at least 98% of the time it will sound like you are just whining. Be specific about what they are doing and how it's a problem. My son complained to me in general terms about a club not being fun for months but it wasn't until he told me that the "coach" blamed him (alone) for the whole team losing a competition in front of the whole team that I understood and agreed it was time for him to quit. (Supposedly, his refusal to smile for a picture led to low scores for "team spirit" and a resulting loss.) If he had told me that after the competition, he wouldn't have gone to a single additional meeting.

If you are in an elite group such as a travel sports team or a club that routinely goes to World's, know that there is a good chance that you need to either do as the coach asks or change activities, no matter what you or your parents think. That isn't always a bad thing. There are people who have medaled at the Olympics who regret not talking about abusive coaches. Looking back, the long-term damage wasn't worth the short-term glory. Changing coaches would have been good for them. (Most cases aren't that extreme, of course, but it is important to talk to a trusted adult for help handling your stress.) Almost anyone who is in the elite for a sport or club has reduced or nearly eliminated other activities to focus on being outstanding in that area. That's normal and your competitor are almost certainly doing the same thing.

There could be another team that is nearly as good but whose style/schedule suits you better. If you have "burnt out" on an activity, moving to a less competitive group can help make it fun again. But if you still love that group, you'll need to find a way to accept that reality. Of course, if you aren't challenged, you might need to look for a more challenging team/group to join.

Sometimes, in small amounts, stress can actually be a good thing. It can motivate and push you to do more than you ever thought you could and that's how good coaches use it. In short bursts (short is the critical word here), it can make you focus mentally, which is helpful in a dangerous situation where situational awareness can use a boost. Nature never intended stress to be a permanent, daily, 24/7 part of our lives. That's when it starts to hurt us.

Aromatherapy (Nice Smells)

This is a fancy way of saying "smell something that makes you feel happy and relaxed." Different things work for different people. A few common ones are cookies baking, flowers, and perfume (especially connected to someone you love, like Grandma). There are other smells that are known to cause most people to feel calmer. Lavender is the most famous of these, but chamomile is another.

Spend a few minutes thinking about what makes you feel calm. Are there any smells associated with it? Are there any smells that you just love without any other association? Many people love the summery scent of freshly cut grass. The oily smell of a garage instantly calms me. The combination of smells reminds me of a mechanic I loved.

Write down all of the smells you like in a list. Take your list and look online for things that smell like that. It might be a perfume, linen spray, a candle, or essential oils. If you can find something with a scent that calms you, buy it and keep it on hand for any time you feel stressed.

Art and Music

Coloring is a trendy calming activity but all kinds of art and music can be great ways to calm yourself. The creative process uses different parts of your mind and that can be very soothing. Equally important, repetition can be calming and soothing, and a lot of art requires repetition. The repetition of a pencil, pen, or brush going back and forth until the page or canvas is fully colored. The repetition of replacing one pencil or brush and choosing a new one. The repetition of practicing a piece of music or a phrase that is repeated in music you listen to. The repetition of practicing a dance.

Take the time to enjoy art. Look at books. Listen to new kinds of music. Maybe you won't like it but every now and then there is a surprise. Cable and the internet both provide tons of options for free music, so there is no excuse that you can't find any good music to listen to. Major museums around the world have digitized much of their collections and many pieces can be downloaded for free. You can make your own selection of world-class artwork to use for screensavers and backgrounds, even at an Arctic Research Base.

If you are looking for beautiful natural images, take a few minutes to look through the websites in the Resources section for this chapter. The US Geological Survey, in particular, has truly stunning images. Scrolling through the images can feel like wasting time, or acting childish, but it isn't.

Next time you feel stressed, give art a chance.

Calm Breathing

When any animal, including humans, is in danger, they run. Running leads to running out of breath–breathing with fast, shallow breaths. Panic has a similar effect. When you are breathing that way and haven't been exercising hard, your body naturally thinks you are in danger and starts the fight or flight response. To combat this, take long, deep, slow breaths. After a minute or two, you should be able to feel your body relaxing. Your heart should stop beating so hard and your mind shouldn't be racing any more as your breathing returns to normal.

There is no reason to wait until you are highly stressed to start calm breathing. As soon as you start to feel anxious, take a few deep breaths.

Charity/Volunteering

Help someone else. Seeing how bad things can get just might make you feel better about your own situation. Helping others has been shown to lower stress levels in people who volunteer. In an odd quirk, your mind and body know your intention. If you aren't genuinely motivated to help others, you're probably better off trying another way to lower your stress.

Hopefully helping someone else will make you feel better too!

Get Outside

Your Mom isn't wrong when she tells you to turn off the electronics and go outside. The whole family should. Being outside has demonstrated massive mental and physical benefits so get outside, unless allergy or other concerns prevent it. Gardening is good for you even if you don't plan anything edible, even if it's a little apartment container garden.

Give it a try. What's the worst that could happen?

Meditating

We have all seen images of people meditating. The classic pose is someone either sitting crisscross-applesauce or in Lotus position with the back of their open hands resting on their knees. (Lotus position is like crisscross-applesauce except your feet are on top of your thighs instead of underneath.) Meditation doesn't actually require a specific position. Sure, Lotus is a great position for it but meditating is about your mental state not your body position. You can walk and meditate or cook and meditate. Really, if you can zone out while you do it, you can meditate while you do it.

To meditate, find a quiet place where you won't be disturbed and that feels at least somewhat peaceful to you. If you decide to do walking meditation, choose a larger space and walk through it as you meditate. If you are sitting, sit crisscross applesauce or in Lotus.

You can set a timer to go off (preferably quietly) when your time is finished. If you like meditation, there are apps specifically designed as meditation timers that have soothing, peaceful tones for the timer. This is much easier than trying to watch the clock, which can't help but be distracting.

How long should you meditate? Aim for one minute for every year old you are. If you can do more, great! If you aren't quite there yet, you'll work up to it. And if you don't have time, do as much as you can fit in.

Empty your mind as much as possible. Pay attention to the breath going in and out of your body. Let go of your thoughts, your worries, and your fears. Notice the sounds around you. Feel what the space is like (temperature, breezes, the surface under you, etc.). The goal is to not concentrate on anything. Let thoughts flow out as quickly as they flow in.

Don't get mad at yourself if your mind doesn't empty and stay that way. It takes a lot of practice. One of the lovely things about meditation (other than being able to do it literally anywhere) is that it benefits you even if you are distracted, just not quite as much.

Physical Activity

Get up and get moving! Run! Skip! Practice martial arts! Play a video game that requires movement! Spin around in circles in the yard! Run through sprinklers! Do burpees! Whatever it is, spend at least 10-20 minutes exercising and moving around. By the time you are done, a lot of stress and other hard emotions should have melted away, especially if you spend time outdoors. (No promises that all of it will, but a noticeable amount should.)

If you are really tense, hitting or kicking a punching bag can be an outstanding way to work off some of the tension. After you have pounded out some of your frustration, things really do feel better most of the time.

Slow Down

While you are at it, think about slowing down your life in general. When your family is rushing around doing last-minute things before taking a trip–even just one to the grocery store–are they calmer or more stressed? What does that tell you about rushing around? Perhaps that rushing around makes it harder to be calm?

If it is your brain and thoughts that are rushing, try your calm breathing. When our thoughts rush too much, it is impossible to think through the situation because we miss too many details in all that hurrying. If you are rushing because you are over-scheduled, think about whether you really want to be in all those things then talk to your parents. Maybe you can scale back some of it.

If you have to go along on a ton of things for other family members, maybe you can find a way to stay home more often. Agreeing to help with laundry, making dinner, or another chore is a good way to get parental buy-in. You may be skeptical but think about it this way: You spend a total of fifteen minutes doing a couple loads of laundry. In exchange, you get ninety minutes at home instead of running errands and watching your sisters karate class. Not such a bad deal.

Sensory (Touching and Smelling)

Some things just feel so nice that touching them is soothing. In our house, we have small "Zen gardens" to play with when stressed. They are simply resealable kitchen containers filled with a soothing color of craft sand and some of the smooth colored rocks you can buy at tourist places. It's almost possible to feel stress slip away from your body as the soft sand runs through your fingers.

Physical touch can help as well. Sometimes just sitting so you are touching someone you love and trust, like a parent, can be very calming. It doesn't need to be much–sticking out a foot or hand to rest against them, barely touching, or stopping to rest a hand on the top of their head for a few moments may be enough to help. Other times, an extended full bear-hug is required.

One odd thing that can help is a weighted blanket. You can buy or make one but for some people, having a heavy blanket (weight not warmth) is extremely calming. For that matter, a heated electric blanket or throw can have the same effect but they don't last as long and aren't as portable since electricity is required to use them.

The Worst That Could Happen

Think about the worst that could happen if what you fear actually happens. Not the kind of worst, not sort of bad–the *worst*. Is it even remotely possible that will happen? Is the next-to-worst likely? What really is likely?

One summer, I was most of the way through an aerial adventure park when I caught up to a boy and his father. The boy was afraid to cross the last few elements. I talked him through making his way across one while his dad waited behind him. (Only one person is allowed on the element at a time.) I zoomed ahead. Right before I left, I saw he was paralyzed with fear and couldn't go on. I tried talking to him again but he was too afraid. I finally asked him, "What are you afraid of? What do you think will happen?"

He thought about it. He didn't say he would fall–the harnesses would prevent that. He didn't say he would hit his head or otherwise injure himself–his dad wouldn't have had him up there if it was dangerous. After he though through all of this, he finally looked up at me and admitted the truth, "Nothing." Once he thought through the possibilities, all those terrible things his mind was trying to tell him might happen, he knew they wouldn't and then he was afraid of…nothing. He zoomed over and finished the course.

That is how many things are. If we stop to think, if we don't let our emotions totally overwhelm us, we can see that we are literally afraid of nothing.

Activity

Spend five minutes meditating three times in one week. And the next time you feel yourself getting mad, practice your deep breathing.

Quick Quiz

T/F   Meditation is useless unless you do it for hours at a time.

T/F   No one can calm themselves in the middle of a crowd.

T/F   Stress is never helpful.

T/F   If you calm yourself and get upset again, there is no point in calming your body a second time.

T/F   Most adults are good at remaining calm.

Resources

Articles

4 Basic Sources of Stress
www.mindfulnessmuse.com/stress-reduction/what-are-the-4-basic-sources-of-stress

Anti-Stress Hacks
wakayaperfection.com/blogs/wellness/18149985-these-anti-stress-hacks-just-might-change-your-life

Aromatherapy Recipes for Calming and Relaxing
birchhillhappenings.com/recipes/calm.htm

Exercise and Stress: Get Moving to Manage Stress
www.mayoclinic.org/healthy-lifestyle/stress-management/in-depth/exercise-and-stress/art-20044469

How to be a Calm Person
www.psychologytoday.com/us/blog/the-creativity-cure/201402/how-be-calm-person

Mental Benefits of Art are for Everyone
bebrainfit.com/the-health-benefits-of-art-are-for-everyone/

The Positive Effects of Stress
www.healthguidance.org/entry/15537/1/The-Positive-Effects-of-Stress.html

Stress Management—Effects of Stress
www.webmd.com/balance/stress-management/stress-management-effects-of-stress

Volunteering and Its Surprising Health Benefits
www.helpguide.org/articles/healthy-living/volunteering-and-its-surprising-benefits.htm/

Volunteering May be Good for Body and Mind
www.health.harvard.edu/blog/volunteering-may-be-good-for-body-and-mind-201306266428

Why Gardening is Good for Your Health
www.cnn.com/2011/HEALTH/07/08/why.gardening.good/index.html

Books

365 Meditations for Teens by Sally Sharpe

Craft to Heal by Nancy Monson

The Relaxation and Stress Reduction Workbook for Teens by Michael Tompkins, PhD and Jonathan Barkin, PsyD (part of a series)

Image Resources

Many museums have images available online for **personal** use.

Library of Congress
www.loc.gov/pictures/

National Park Service Photos
www.nps.gov/aboutus/news/photosmultimedia.htm

The Smithsonian Image Collection
sirismm.si.edu/siris/sirisimagegallery.htm

The Smithsonian Photo Collection
siarchives.si.edu/what-we-do/photograph-and-image-collections

US Department of the Interior Photos
www.doi.gov/photos

US Geological Survey Multimedia Gallery
www.usgs.gov/products/multimedia-gallery/overview

Other

Adult coloring books

Be Mindful Card Deck for Teens

Essential oil diffusers: room, car, necklace, and more are available

Herbal supplements: stress soothing formula

Lavender in pretty much any form you can smell

Stress balls including musical ones from Asia

Weighted blanket

Videos

5 Reasons Teens are More Stressed Than Adults
www.youtube.com/watch?v=Scot0rJGtUA

How to Meditate for Children: A Kids Guide to Peace
www.youtube.com/watch?v=98ficcEu-ns

How to Meditate for Children #2: Colour Meditation
www.youtube.com/watch?v=hXpTBZLEtQc

How to Meditate for Children #3: Love
www.youtube.com/watch?v=fTBL4qQVWUg

LIVE IT: Spiritual Health Improves Physical & Mental Quality
www.youtube.com/watch?v=ZpQfo2_I-ug

Managing Stress: Brainsmart BBC
www.youtube.com/watch?v=hnpQrMqDoqE

{FIVE}

PRESSURE

Sometimes the worst dangers come from people we know in real life, sometimes even ones we are told to trust. They may try to pressure us to do things we don't want to. They may be adults or old people or our peers, or even younger than us. Whatever their age, it's not OK. If someone tells you, "You'll get in big trouble if you tell what I did," the truth is almost certainly that *they* will get in big trouble, possibly even go to jail, if you tell someone and they believe you. (If you tell someone and they don't, tell someone else, and keep trying until you find someone who believes you.)

What kind of things should you "tell" about? It's fairly simple: if it makes you feel uncomfortable or scared or feels wrong, then tell. When you talk to an adult you trust, they can help figure out if there is a real problem, a misunderstanding, or just different expectations. It might be scary to know that a person could get in big trouble if you tell on them, but if they hurt one person, they will probably hurt another. You are helping not just yourself but other people. Even if the problem is a misunderstanding and nothing that gets anyone in big trouble, it may still be good to talk about it so they don't upset anyone else and so you aren't upset anymore either.

Unfortunately, this isn't just something that happens to kids. I'm an adult and I've been bullied by other adults. I tried telling other adults who could have helped. They thought it was no big deal and blew it off. It kept going. Others blew it off, but some saw the problem. While they couldn't help, at least I didn't feel like I was imagining things or blowing them out of proportion anymore. Finally, I found someone who believed me. By this time, I wasn't the only victim. But we all worked together and it finally stopped, because I was willing to keep trying until I found someone to help. There is no denying it's hard to keep trying when people don't believe you or don't think it's important. It's your choice whether you fight it or not.

Code Words (or Phrases)

It's a great idea to set up "code words" (or phrases) in advance so you can tell your parents, or another person you trust, that you need help without letting the people physically near you know. For example, if your parents know any mention of your "purple hoodie" means to come get you *immediately*, it's easy to slip that into a conversation. The other people around you will have no clue that you don't *own* a purple hoodie (or whatever), so they won't be suspicious.

There are a few reasons you might not want others to know if you ask for help. First, it might be embarrassing, especially if you are with friends who are pressuring you to do something. Second, you might not be sure if something is OK or not, and that can make calling for help embarrassing. Third, and least likely, it could be unsafe if people near you knew you were calling for help.

Pressure (Peer and Otherwise)

Peer pressure has a bad rap for always being *bad*. The truth is, it can go either way. If 22 kids in a classroom are attentive and care about getting grades that are good enough for college, and one student keeps trying to distract the rest, they have a chance to use peer pressure to get that student on the right track. Peers can also make you feel lousy when you act like a jerk.

Peers aren't the only ones who pressure us, though. Parents, teachers, coaches, club advisors, grandparents, bosses.... Most of the time, pressure exists to help us go where we need to be, but sometimes it goes too far or pushes us to do (or accept) the wrong thing.

Good Pressure

If two people have a friendly rivalry that causes them both to push a little harder, do a little more, learn a little more, that can be good pressure. It can lead each of them to be more successful, if it doesn't go too far. If feedback from friends causes a person to be a better team player, that's good pressure. Unfortunately, it's easy for good pressure to be taken too far and then it turns into bad pressure. Sometimes it's a desire for the best possible outcome, even when that outcome isn't realistically possible, or for perfection, which is never really possible. (There is always something that can be nit-picked, even on the most seemingly perfect thing.)

Bad Pressure

Lying, cheating, breaking the rules, hurting others: people are pressured to do things they know are wrong all the time, adults as well as kids. It can be very hard to resist, especially when a group or authority figure (teacher, boss, even parent) pressures you.

There really aren't any easy answers. Unless you are able to physically leave the area, whoever is pressuring you will probably continue to do so until you give in or, possibly, they find a new target. Leaving isn't always possible and doesn't always stop the problem, of course, but if it's an ongoing problem, take the time to really think about how you might be able to rearrange your schedule so you aren't around that person or group. Perhaps you need to take a different route between activities, or change your activities altogether. The Psychology Today article listed in the Resources for Chapter 4 has a great discussion of how this can happen.

Talking to a trusted adult is always a good idea. Sometimes you may need to "report them" to their boss or another adult but this can backfire, making them angry, which is why it's important to talk to a trusted adult first. They may have a way to help you find proof, others with similar experiences, and generally help ensure you are heard. Of course, if you feel they are dangerous, you need to report them as soon as possible, but talk it over with an adult first if you can.

Simply staying busy is another way to avoid pressure. Like leaving the area, if you aren't there, others can't pressure you if you aren't there. Part time jobs, sports, clubs, extra classes, and volunteer work are all great ways to get away and be in an environment that is hopefully healthier.

Conforming

It isn't just peers who pressure us to conform. Parents, teachers, really all the adults in our lives, tend to pressure us to conform. Some of that is a good thing. After a few years, everyone is expected to use the potty for toileting needs. Conforming to that expectation is a good thing. Everyone is required to wears shoes into restaurants and wash their hands frequently if they work with food. That is also a good thing for health and hygiene reasons.

But sometimes people around us, adults and kids, pressure us to conform in ways that make us uncomfortable. Sometimes, conforming is about what adults remember from their childhood, or what kids see on TV, in books or in movies. Those expectations may have nothing to do with your life, right now. For example, where I live now, there is *a lot* of Nerd Pride. The kids seem to compete to see who can do the nerdiest activities. Some parents might think nerdy activities would cause their child to get atomic wedgies every day, based on their childhood, when that simply isn't true here. Kids may have to work hard to get their parents to understand why their choice is OK, and it may not work. Parents (grandparents, aunts, uncles) just may not be able to understand that the robotics team really is more prestigious than the football team. That's just how it goes sometimes, as much as no one likes to hear that.

Be yourself. There is no one else you can be.

Too Much Touch

Sometimes, we all feel pressured to accept touching we don't really want. Not all touching is bad, even from people who are way too touchy-feely, even when we don't want it. Sometimes a doctor, parent, or other adult needs to touch you to check for injuries or to keep you safe. Sometimes old people like to touch a lot and they don't mean anything wrong by it. That doesn't make it OK for them to touch you, especially without asking, when you really don't want to, but it does need to be dealt with differently than someone who wants to do Bad Things.

That's another reason it's important to talk to an adult you trust if someone does something that makes you uncomfortable: They will have a better idea of which ones are dangerous and which are just uncomfortable. If it's someone your parents know, they can tell you if your huggy and touchy Grand-Uncle is harmless, or a creep everyone avoids. If Grand-Uncle is harmless, then maybe it will help you feel OK with a bit more touching than you accept from most people. If you still don't (and it's OK either way), then work with your parents or someone else to figure out a way to steer clear of him. Obviously, if he's a creep, they should help you steer clear of Grand-Uncle entirely.

This point needs to be very clear: It's not OK for anyone to force you to accept touching you don't want, unless it is literally to save a life. With that said, think about the intent and what accepting the touch will cost you. If the only cost to you is only momentary mild discomfort and it reassures someone who loves you, or provides comfort to a lonely friend or relative, perhaps you can accept it for their sake. Grandparents and other elderly people, in particular, are often isolated and a nice hug can do wonders for them.

If your mom is hugging you but you think you are too grown up, why do you *really* think she is doing it? You know, in your heart, when there is no ill intent. Your mom loves you. What does it hurt you to accept that show of affection and even return it? On the other hand, if you know she is trying to control you and keep you a little kid, well, good luck with that. (That's not a snarky comment; it's a genuine acknowledgement of how hard it can be when parents are unwilling to let their kids grow up because there is not much a kid of any age can do about it.)

Activity

Set up a code word or phrase to use with your family.

Quick Quiz

T/F   Handshakes are a form of physical touch we usually need to accept, even if it feels uncomfortable (but only our right hand).

T/F   It is always OK for people to touch us as much as they want, whether we are OK with it or not.

T/F   Peer pressure is always bad.

T/F   Code words can be a good thing.

T/F   Pressure to do things and conform only comes from peers.

Resources

Articles

How Positive Peer Pressure Works
www.secureteen.com/peer-pressure/how-positive-peer-pressure-works

BE CALM AND HANDLE STRESS

Interview Question: How Do You Handle Stress?
www.thebalancecareers.com/how-do-you-handle-stress-2061246

NBA Encyclopedia: Handling the Pressure
www.nba.com/encyclopedia/finals/Handling_Pressure.html

How to Handle Pressure
www.wikihow.com/Handle-Pressure

Books

Daily Reflections for Highly Effective Teens by Sean Covey

Enough as She Is: How to Help Girls Move Beyond Impossible Standards of Success to Live Healthy, Happy, and Fulfilling Lives by Rachel Simmons

How to Say NO and Keep Your Friends: Peer Pressure Reversal for Teens and Preteens by Sharon Scott

Performing Under Pressure: The Science of Doing Your Best When it Matters Most by Hendrie Weisinger and J.P. Pawliw-Fry

Under Pressure: Confronting the Epidemic of Stress and Anxiety in Girls by Lisa Damour, Ph.D.

A Young Man's Guide to Making Right Choices: Your Life God's Way by Jim George

Scouting-Specific

A Time to Tell Troop Meeting Guide (BSA)
www.scouting.org/filestore/pdf/46-180.pdf

Videos

How to Handle Pressure as an Entrepreneur
www.youtube.com/watch?v=0NUHEOkfMFo

How to Stay Calm When You Know You'll be stressed | Daniel Levitin
www.youtube.com/watch?v=8jPQjjsBbIc

{PART 2}
FINANCIAL SAVVY AND WORK

These are some of the most basic things an adult must learn to be able to function effectively in our modern world. If you can't manage your money, then you run out of it more quickly and get into a lot of trouble.

The Basics–Budgeting, Saving, and Spending Money: This is possibly the most basic, foundational step of all. While simple, it isn't easy.

Negotiating (Bargaining and Trading): In most first-world countries, it doesn't seem like bargaining and trading are really part of our daily lives, but they are still there. EBay or yard sales, anyone? They are also there when we do comparison shopping and when we trade-in used items for store credit or cash.

Storing and Hiding Assets: This brings to mind pirates gold, vaults behind paintings, and bank accounts in Switzerland and the Cayman Islands, but it really is simpler than that. When you have valuable items in your home, how do you keep them safely hidden?

Starting and Ending a Job: Everyone gets new jobs and eventually leaves them, even if it's by retiring. It's just part of life. How you do this can impact what your boss (and coworkers) think of you, the opportunities you receive, and what kind of references you receive.

Manners: It may sound old-fashioned, but manners matter. They really are the grease that makes life run more smoothly.

{SIX}

THE BASICS

No matter how rich or poor they may be, every person has times that they have more, or less, money. There also comes a time in every person's life when their parents stop paying the bills and they have to do it themselves. This is usually gradual, starting with non-essentials like movie tickets and eventually progressing to include food, heat, shelter, medical, and everything else.

Depending on how good your money management skills are, these financial ebbs and flows can be more or less painful. If you don't develop good money management skills before you start handling your own finances, you could easily run out of money and not have enough to pay for basic essentials like food and shelter, much less modern essentials such as transportation and insurance. Even a small loss of income can ruin your vacation plans or leave you unable to buy new music you want.

Budgeting

Budgeting is the process of determining how much money you have and what you will do with it, and it's critical for financial well-being. The first step is to determine your income—all the money you have coming in. The next is figure out your expenditures—how much you spend. This is harder. A lot of expenses are small but a few dollars for snacks, another few for new gym shorts, and a little more for a tasty beverage definitely adds up, especially if you do it regularly.

The truly hard part is making sure your expenditures aren't greater than your income. When they are greater, you go into debt. When they are less, you can save money, as long as you don't start spending more because you have it in your account. It's a good idea to move that money from your regular checking account to a savings account or somewhere else that you won't see it and be tempted to spend it.

To figure out where all your money is going, keep a notepad with you every day and record every time you spend or receive even a penny, noting what it was for. Doing this for one week may be enough, or you may need to continue to do it for a month, depending on how regular your schedule and bills are. If you only do it for one week, be sure it's a fairly "normal" week, not a holiday week. Include any recurring bills you may have (car insurance, gas, lunch) and think about any one-time upcoming expenses you may have (trips, gifts). You need to include those expenses in your budget.

Once you have all the numbers, enter them into a spreadsheet or app and total them. If you use automated totaling, it will update the total whenever you update your expenditures or income. Expenditures and income should "balance" so you don't spend more than you receive, or (better yet) leave you with money you can save. The goal is to have more money coming in than you have going out. This money can be saved, given to charity, used to pay down old bills, or invested.

Spending more than you receive is either "running a deficit" or "going into debt" and can't be sustained for long. Look to see where you can either lower expenses or increase your income, but know that lowering your expenses is almost always easier. If you are running a deficit, then you are either spending money you worked hard to save or are going into debt.

There are times when this cannot be avoided, such as when a company downsizes and their employees lose their jobs, resulting in no income until they have a new job. Most adults have been laid off, fired, or otherwise forced to leave a job when they didn't want to at some point. This is reality, and adults (even young adults) need to prepare for it both by saving money and by having things they can use even if they lose their job. Some people build a "deep pantry" of long-term storage food they can use in an emergency. This is discussed more in *Chapter 9: Starting and Ending a Job.*

If you do an online search for "budgeting", it quickly becomes clear that there are a lot of different methods for doing this. If your first (second, fifteenth) attempt fails, keep the parts that work and keep tweaking it until it works. For example, one blogger figured out that she was trying to use monthly templates but she's paid weekly. Doing weekly budgeting works better for her. She kept at it until she figured out what works for her.

Charity

Helping others is important. There are two basic kinds of charity. Some benefit a cause (saving the rainforests) and others focus on people in need (food banks).

Charities that benefit people focus on those who don't have enough money to meet their basic needs or who fit a specific category, such as having a specific illness or being veterans. Some of those who are being helped made bad choices and things got so bad they need help to become self-reliant again. Others have hit bad times for reasons beyond their ability to control, like the Great Depression. Still others simply had bad luck, such as a person with a genetic disease or who was exposed to something toxic on the job.

Earning money takes hard work, so why spend that money on someone else? The top reasons are to fix a problem and to make yourself feel good. (Please do note that you shouldn't donate so much to charity that you can't pay your own bills, although that should go without saying.) Which problem depends on what you are interested in because no matter what your interest, there is a charity related to it. Most people feel good when they help others by donating money or time (volunteering) to charity, but if you are looking for something more concrete, you may also be able to develop skills and gain experience that helps in your life. When you start volunteering, you will probably be given the simplest jobs that need the least skill. As people higher up get to know you better and see that you are a hard worker, they will give you more responsibility and more complex tasks. As an added bonus, as discussed in Chapter Four, volunteering has been demonstrated to help the volunteer's mental health, and often their physical health as well.

If you take the time to genuinely become involved and be an asset to a charity, you can gain experience that looks good on your resume when you are looking for a job, applying for college, or just about anything where they need to see your work history. You may also meet people who will open doors that you otherwise might not even know existed. Volunteering for a charity can (and should) be a win-win.

Helping others matters.

Checking and Savings

These are often connected accounts. If you overdraw your checking—write checks or initiate electronic transfers for more money than you have in your account—many banks simply transfer money between accounts, if there is enough and you have agreed to it. If there isn't enough, they may pay it anyway but charge you a not-insignificant fee. Checking is used to pay the bills and savings is, oddly enough, intended as a place to save money.

Technological changes in the internet era have definitely changed how people use these accounts. Where physical checks were once used to pay almost every bill, including paychecks, many bills are now paid with credit cards and the credit cards are, in turn, paid by an electronic transfer from a checking account, with no paper ever having changed hands. Physical paychecks are rarely issued today with most people choosing to have automatic deposits directly to their bank account, including payments from government agencies such as Social Security. This eliminates the possibility of someone stealing it in the mail and also ensures it is deposited promptly with no need to run out to the bank.

Credit Cards

Credit cards can be used instead of cash most places in the United States. When you use a credit card, you are essentially borrowing money and promising to pay it back later. If you pay it by the monthly due date back, you probably won't have to pay anything for it. If, however, you do not pay off the full amount every month, you will have to pay interest. If you pay after the due date, you will have to pay a penalty.

The credit card company takes a day or two to be sure they have received all the charges against your card up to and including the last day in the statement period (the day the statement closes) and then sends a bill to the cardholder. The monthly due date is generally approximately two to three weeks after the statement closes. Every credit card has an interest rate attached to it, and a grace period. If the bill is paid in full within the grace period—by the due date—then no interest is charged and you have essentially borrowed the money for free. If it is partially paid, then they charge interest on the rest until your card is paid in full. If no payment is made at all, then you have to pay a penalty (late charge) in addition to interest.

Don't skip a payment. The bill will show a minimum due and you need to at least pay that. You may have a $20 minimum payment, but not paying that could easily lead to a $25 late fee. Risking that simply doesn't make any sense. Late payments also look bad on your credit score.

Debit Cards

Unlike credit cards, debit cards take money directly out of your account. If you don't already have money in your account, you can't use a debit card. Be very, very careful not to lose your debit card because it can be used to take all the money from your account.

Treat debit card transactions just like writing checks (or transferring funds electronically), especially if the debit card is attached to your checking account. The bank might take money from one account to cover another if you overdraw one account (spend more than you have). For example, if you have $300 in checking, write a check for $178 to pay your credit card, mail it to your credit card company, but use your debit card to withdraw $150 before the check to your credit card company clears (is paid), your bank will allow you to withdraw the $150, but then the check for the credit card will bounce. Depending on the bank policies, they may take it from another (attached) account or charge extra fees to cover what is really a short-term, unsecured loan.

You cannot assume that there is money in the account. It is 100% your responsibility to keep track of how much you have deposited and how much you have spent/withdrawn from your account. It is 0% (zero percent) the responsibility of the bank, or your family. Since a debit card only works if there is money in the account, you cannot really overdraw a debit card, although you can overdraw the account it is tied to, like in the checking account example above.

Credit Score

Your credit score shows whether you do a good job or bad job with your money based on specific criteria banks and other institutions can check, such as whether you pay your bills on time. Two key factors are how much debt you have and your declared income because they need to know you can repay any loan offered to you. (If you are paid in cash or goods, that doesn't count toward your credit score.)

A low credit score makes it hard to get credit in the form of credit cards, car loans, or a mortgage. Any credit you do receive will be at a higher interest rate (making it more expensive) and may include extra requirements such as carrying extra insurance. On the other end of the scale, an excellent credit rating may enable you to get 0% interest for credit cards and car loans.

Oddly enough, having no credit cards doesn't make your credit score go up. Having one or more credit cards *but not going anywhere near your spending limit* is one of the best ways to improve your credit score. One recommendation is to be at or below 30 % of your credit limit, called your credit utilization. That means that if your credit cards have a limit of $1,000, you shouldn't have more than $300 on them after you make your monthly payments. (Fully paying them off is by far the best choice.)

The credit agencies look at the average age of your accounts. That means opening a bunch of new cards you don't plan to use to improve your credit utilization could backfire. It also means that if you have an account that was opened for you by your parents in junior high, it's a good idea to keep it even if you are now 50 rarely use it. I have one like that with an interest rate that is higher than I accept on a new card, but since I've had it for nearly 30 years, it helps my credit score.

Credit scores are important, take time to build, and can be hard to understand. The short version is don't carry much debt and pay your bills on time, every time.

Activity

With your parents' help, list all the income you normally receive during the year. Include allowance, birthday gifts, holiday gifts, and any special occasions (like a Quinceañera or graduation) that may lead to presents. Separate the ones that you know you will get (paychecks), from the ones you *might* get (presents) and from ones that depend on how well you do (bonuses for good grades).

How much of your "income" are you sure of? How much depends on choices others make, such as whether to give you money or an item as a gift? How much depends on how well you do your job (getting good grades, listening to your parents, doing chores)?

Talk to your parents or another adult about whether adult income is partially dependent on choices others make and how well they do their job. Do *not* expect them to give you specific dollar amounts or percentages; if they want to, that's OK, but it's personal information they probably won't share.

Quick Quiz

T/F   Credit cards withdraw money directly from your bank account.

T/F   Good credit is important, especially for big purchases.

T/F   Checking and saving accounts are usually linked together.

T/F   Donating to charity can be a win-win.

T/F   Good budgeting skills are critical for financial well-being.

Resources

Articles

5 Surprising Benefits of Volunteering
www.forbes.com/sites/nextavenue/2015/03/19/5-surprising-benefits-of-volunteering/#67b67c2127bf

Charity Watch (shows how well charities use donated funds)
www.charitywatch.org

Debit & Credit: 2 Very Different Cards
www.youtube.com/watch?v=JO2xf_8TLLY

*How a Debit Card Works (also explains credit cards)
www.thebalance.com/what-is-a-debit-card-2385853

How do Debit Cards Work (technical description)
www.bankrate.com/banking/swipe-how-do-debit-cards-work/

How a FICO Credit Score is Determined |Continuing Education
www.youtube.com/watch?v=JO2xf_8TLLY

How to Repair Your Credit Score
www.myfico.com/credit-education/improve-your-credit-score

These 4 Steps Will Teach You How to Budget (Finally)
www.moneyunder30.com/no-more-budgets

What is a Credit Score?
www.myfico.com/credit-education/credit-scores

What is the range for credit scores?
www.nerdwallet.com/blog/finance/credit-score-ranges-and-how-to-improve

Your Credit Score: The Secret Formula Behind That Magic Number
www.rd.com/advice/saving-money/your-credit-score-the-magic-money-number-explained

Books

Broke Millennial: Stop Scraping By and Get Your Financial Life Together by Erin Lowry

How Money Works: The Facts Visually Explained by DK

How to Manage Your Money When You Don't Have Any by Erik Wecks

Is Plastic Money Real? How Credit Cards Work by Baby Professor

This Might be a Dumb Question but…How Does Money Work? By Joe Fazio

The Minimalist Budget: A Practical Guide On How to Save Money, Spend Less and Live More With a Minimalist Lifestyle By Simeon Lindstrom

Other

Budget Planner

Budget Planning and Budget Instructions (worksheets)
www.moneyinstructor.com/budgeting.asp

Cash Envelopes and Budget Planning

Give, Save, Spend Cash Envelopes

Scouting-Specific

American Business Merit Badge
meritbadge.org/wiki/index.php/American_Business

Budgeting Badge
forgirls.girlscouts.org/home/badgeexplorer/#budgeting

Business Owner Badge
forgirls.girlscouts.org/home/badgeexplorer/#business-owner

Buying Power Badge
forgirls.girlscouts.org/home/badgeexplorer/#buying-power

Good Credit
forgirls.girlscouts.org/home/badgeexplorer/#good-credit

Money Manager Badge
forgirls.girlscouts.org/home/badgeexplorer/#money-manager

On My Own Badge
forgirls.girlscouts.org/home/badgeexplorer/#on-my-own

Personal Management Merit Badge
meritbadge.org/wiki/index.php/Personal_Management

Savvy Shopper Badge
forgirls.girlscouts.org/home/badgeexplorer/#savvy-shopper

Videos

Budgeting for Beginners – How to Budget
www.youtube.com/watch?v=fOpSiQetTy4

The Budgeting Method That Changed My Life
www.youtube.com/watch?v=HGRLEi-93pQ

HOW TO Budget Money As A Teen
www.youtube.com/watch?v=JO2xf_8TLLY

Teenager/Small Income Budget! (envelope stuffing)
www.youtube.com/watch?v=_PKyqG88k-U

{SEVEN}

NEGOTIATING

The ability to value something, and then bargain and/or trade for it has been prized since the start of human existence. If you ask them, most people will tell you they don't do these things in their modern daily life. But many really do. Craigslist and eBay are prime examples.

Looking at items in the store or online and deciding if the price is fair, or one you are willing to pay, is just another form of this. Jewelry at Tiffany's may be fairly priced for the amount of detailed craftsmanship, but it is also definitely more than I am willing to pay. When you are at a park in the summer heat and someone rolls through with ice cold water for $1.50 or more a bottle—water you *know* costs $4.00 for a case of 24 at the store—there is a very good chance you will buy it because it is worth the extra cost to stay at the park, and because you will get dehydrated if you don't drink enough. Then you won't be able to have fun at all until you recover, most likely another day.

When you are trading with another person, no matter what form it takes, the way you act toward them can affect the final price. If you insult them or their products, or offer too little money, they may refuse to give you a really good deal. If you are nice to them, you may get a better offer than they were originally planning on offering. In any event, good manners never hurt. This is true even in big purchases and when the price is set. How could you get more if the price is set? Simple: Sometimes companies have incentives you don't know about. A salesperson who feels kindly toward you might give you a coupon or tell you about an upcoming sale. They might also throw in an extra item, most often in the form of samples. One time when our son was small, a salesperson mentioned that they could give us a toddler-size version of the car we were looking at if they salesperson really wanted to seal the deal!

Bartering (and Haggling)

In many parts of the world, people barter with farmers and shopkeepers every day when they buy their food and other items. For most of us, the only time we barter outside of markets on international vacations are flea markets and yard sales.

Bartering is when people exchange two goods directly with no money involved. Haggling is when the buyer and seller go back and forth on price, although it is also commonly called bartering. The seller offers a price, then the buyer offers a lower price(a counteroffer). They go back and forth on price until they finally agree on one. It is possible that one person will never budge and will get their price (often indicated by saying the price is "firm"), but it is usually somewhere in the middle.

In the modern US, the most common places for bartering (outside of yard sales and flea markets) are, believe it or not, our largest purchases: homes and cars. There is information online to help figure out what those items are worth so you can make a good first offer and know what a good price is, but if you really make the seller angry (or if you make them think you're a fool who will pay anything for their item), then you'll get a worse deal.

NEGOTIATING

Seasonal Value

Sometimes items are worth more than others. Scarcity and demand determine much of that change, as with cold bottled water being worth more in the middle of a hot field. Much of this change is seasonal and is the same every year. You can see this seasonal change in action at the grocery store. When corn is being harvested, there is a lot of fresh corn. The price drops because it is plentiful. Other times of the year, it has to be trucked in. There isn't as much of it available and transport costs are higher. The same is true with everything else in the produce department.

EBay is another good place to see seasonal price changes in action. Toys sell for more from late November to just before Christmas because people are buying Christmas gifts. In January-February, the prices drop like a rock because people just finished buying a lot of toys and they have to pay off their credit card debt from Christmas.

Value in a Disaster

In a disaster, items that normally don't have much value can become extremely valuable. Different kinds of emergencies lead to different specific items having value, such as water pumps having more value in a flood and sand/ice melt in an ice storm. Although ice storms are normally small and don't have much effect, they can shut down entire cities for an extended period of time.

Batteries, candles, and generators are all examples of items that can have a great deal of value in a power outage that don't in a normal situation. (Power outages are common in all kinds of emergencies.) Flashlights, lanterns, radios, and all manner of small gadgets require batteries but many people do not check them regularly. They let the batteries die and don't replace them, and they don't have extras on hand to see them through a long period of lots of use.

Negotiating a Salary

It is true, most salaries have a range and can be negotiated, but know that you will never earn big bucks flipping burgers. Once you get beyond the most entry-level jobs with no skills required, most have some flexibility, and high-level jobs have even more flexibility through what is called a "benefits package." This includes vacation time, health insurance, stock options, and quite a variety of other, smaller perks that may be highly specific to the company.

Employers know that if they pay too little, their employees will leave quickly and it is costly to find and train new employees, so most offer a fair salary and compensation–but companies usually make offers on the low side of fair. In order to convince an employer to increase their offer, or to give you a raise later, you need to give them a reason, such as some great (and relevant) work or volunteer experience, specific skills, or training/education/certifications. For example, if you are offered a position at a drug store earning minimum wage in a neighborhood with a large population of elderly Armenians, asking for a higher wage because you speak fluent Armenian is perfectly reasonable, especially if you didn't mention it on your application. It will help you do a better job and will make their customers happy, which is good for the business. If you are an Eagle Scout or earned your Girl Scout Gold Award, those do show a skill set in terms of planning and executing a project and many businesses (including the US military) actually pay more if you earned either of those.

The more specific information you can provide, the better. Salary negotiations are done either with Human Resources (HR) or directly with The Boss. Either way, their goal is to hire you at the lowest salary you are willing to accept as fair, and your goal is to get the highest salary they are willing to pay. Until and unless you have a skill set that is so rare and sought after that you can name your own salary, which pretty much never happens, keep in mind that if you push too hard, they can rescind the offer and you will need to start job-hunting all over again.

I *highly* recommend two books by Linda Babcock and Sara Laschever to help you learn more about negotiating a salary. While they were written specifically for women, they are good for men as well: *Women Don't Ask: The High Cost of Avoiding Negotiation and Positive Strategies for Change* and *Ask for It: How Women Can Use the Power of Negotiation to Get What They Really Want.*

Activity

Go to a yard sale or flea market. Bargain to see what good deals you can get. This can be a competition with each person having a certain amount of money–$20 or so–and whoever gets the best deals wins.

OR

Find something you no longer want or use. After your parents approve and with their help, sell it on eBay, Craigslist, Facebook Marketplace, or a yard sale.

> **Note:** Craigslist is a great place to buy, sell, and trade items, but there can be a **_huge_** Stranger Danger element compared to the other options, no matter how old you are, so be very cautious and make sure an(other) adult is present and involved in every step of the transaction, both online and in the real world. Don't go alone!

Quick Quiz

T/F   Bartering is a normal part of all shopping, including grocery shopping, in many parts of the world

T/F   In bartering, you must accept the other person's first offer.

T/F   Making a first offer that is too low can make the other person mad, which can lead to you either not getting the item or paying a lot more for it.

T/F   Money is always be used in bartering.

T/F   Bartering is only done with strangers.

Resources

Articles

5 Tips to Negotiate Better with Just about Anyone
lifehacker.com/five-tips-to-negotiate-better-with-just-about-anyone-493106085

*How to Get the Best Deals at Garage Sales: Savvy Negotiation Tips
whatmommydoes.com/how-to-get-the-best-deals-at-garage-sales-yard-sale-negotiation-tips

How to Haggle at Flea Markets, Yard Sales, And More
www.thespruce.com/how-to-haggle-1313670

How To Negotiate More Effectively
www.thebalancesmb.com/ways-to-negotiate-more-effectively-2947174

Learn This: How to Negotiate
learnthis.org/negotiate.php

PayScale's Salary Negotiation Guide
www.payscale.com/salary-negotiation-guide

Yard Sale Negotiating: How to Price Items and Make a Profit
www.jugglingmother.net/yard-sale-negotiating-price-items-make-profit

Books

*Ask for It: How Women Can Use the Power of Negotiation to Get What They Really Want by Linda Babcock and Sara Laschever

Bargain with Ease by John A Sarette

Barter Book: How to Protect Yourself When Bartering by Mike Young, Esq.

Getting Past No: Negotiating in Difficult Situations by William Ury

Getting to Yes: Negotiating Agreement Without Giving In by Roger Fisher and William Ury

NEGOTIATING

Haggle and Sell: How to Get Top Dollar for Your Collectibles by Cheryl Kane

Negotiating the Impossible: How to Break Deadlocks and Resolve Ugly Conflicts by Deepak Malhotra

Negotiating the Nonnegotiable: How to Resolve Your Most Emotionally Charged Conflicts by Daniel Shapiro

Ultimate Garage Sales: Your Guides to Having a Hugely Successful and Highly Profitable Garage Sale! By Gregory Quintile

*Women Don't Ask: The High Cost of Avoiding Negotiation and Positive Strategies for Change by Linda Babcock and Sara Laschever

Other

Successful Negotiation: Essential Strategies and Skills (course)
www.coursera.org/learn/negotiation-skills

Scouting-Specific

Comparison Shopping Badge
forgirls.girlscouts.org/home/badgeexplorer/#comparison-shopping

Videos

7 Ways To Improve Your Negotiation Skills
www.youtube.com/watch?v=DZntD2KEJs0

BizKid$: The Art of Negotiation
www.youtube.com/watch?v=GCV2CWIgggM

Conflict Resolution [from BrainPop]
www.youtube.com/watch?v=EABFilCZJy8

Garage Sale Tips: How to Negotiate Yard Sale Pricing
www.youtube.com/watch?v=Do9sY76MVL0

How to Influence People: Persuasion vs. Negotiation Skills
www.youtube.com/watch?v=8E1eV7dMLe4

How to Haggle for a Used Car, an undercover demonstration by Broadcaster Elisabeth Leamy
www.youtube.com/watch?v=UpEsmEaJcJo

Monty Python negotiation Haggle
www.youtube.com/watch?v=-2iZjxSGca8

Negotiation Skills [scenes from *Pirates of the Caribbean*]
www.youtube.com/watch?v=q-0wJGZ_J3I

Salary Negotiation: 6 Tips on How to Negotiate a Higher Salary
www.youtube.com/watch?v=iUAcoetDgH4

{EIGHT}

STORING AND HIDING ASSETS

There are a few kinds of assets people may choose to store and/or hide in their homes. The most obvious are cash and jewelry, but critical paperwork, firearms, and emergency supplies are right near the top of the list as well. My mother in law spent most of her first twenty years of life living in a war zone in one way, shape, or form, including being occupied by a foreign military. She used a safe deposit box for important (and flammable) documents until she was able to keep them in a fire-safe box in her home, but not for cash or valuables. Those she preferred to keep where she could see them and get them more them quickly. When we cleaned out her house, we found an astounding array of items in places no thief would normally look, like the bottom of tissue boxes.

Most of us will never live in a war zone, few people routinely use a safety deposit box today, and even fewer women have valuable "jewels", but most families have at least a few things that are hidden for safekeeping somewhere in their home, most often paperwork like pink slips for cars, passports, and original social security cards. Your family may not be comfortable with you even knowing where to find these things. They may be fine with you knowing where they are but not let you have the keys or code to access them. That's fine too, as long as someone knows where it is or how to find that information if something happens to your parents.

Identity Items

This is probably the most common "asset" people hide today. If another person finds out the social security number, birthday, full legal name, and a few other key details for any person, they can "steal their identity", which basically means pretend they are that person. They can open credit cards and bank accounts in their name, steal money from the real person's bank account, run up debts (which the real person will be responsible for), and much more. For this reason, most people hide their original social security card, passport (including expired passports), old IDs, birth certificates, and other critical documents. People used to use bank safety deposit boxes for this sort of thing, and some still do, but fire safe boxes are a more common choice today. They are lockable, easy to hide, and keep your most important items safe in a fire.

In addition to physical paperwork, you can keep a USB drive with digital backups of important files, family photos, and whatever else matters most to you. Marriage licenses, divorce decrees, custody agreements, lawsuit settlements, wills, name change documents (especially after a marriage or divorce), DNRs (Do Not Resuscitate), and other legal documents should also be kept safe

It's important to shred anything you don't need to keep that has key information such as bank account numbers, social security numbers, medical data, or anything else that is personal. You can't entirely remove the risk of identity theft, but shredding these kinds of documents does reduce it.

STORING AND HIDING ASSETS

Cash and Jewelry

It's a rare woman who doesn't have her jewelry somewhere near where she dresses. However, she may have some more expensive and rarely worn pieces, or family heirlooms (that may mostly have sentimental value), in a safe somewhere else, possibly even a safety deposit box. If they are in the house, they may be hidden to keep them safe. However, part of the reality of life is that most women end up with primarily inexpensive costume jewelry or relatively inexpensive semi-precious gemstones. The one genuinely expensive piece most women have is their engagement ring, and that rarely strays far from her finger and doesn't need any special hiding place.

It is also common to have an "emergency cash stash." If you are a teen and your family does, your parents almost certainly won't tell you how much or where it is, which is fine and normal, but it is important that anyone who is home alone, even for an hour or two, has access to $40-$100 in cash. This might be in your personal piggy bank or it might be emergency cash from your parents. Why that amount? There should be enough to pay for a taxi to the hospital and back because that is probably the most expensive thing you might need to cover. (If you live farther out in the country, you may need more; if you live in an urban area, you may need less or even none.) That should also be enough to pay for a meal if you end up alone longer than expected, if needed.

Anyone reading this probably doesn't need a babysitter, but if you watch a younger sibling, having enough money to pay a sitter if you need to go out before your parents return (or you get home before they do) may come in very handy. You may not ever need it, but it's better to have a small amount of cash on hand, just in case. Just be sure to save it for actual emergencies and let your parents know when you do spend any of it, and why. You don't want to end up with no cash when you most need it.

In certain emergencies, particularly power outages, ATMs and credit cards won't work because they need power. Anyone who already has cash will have an advantage. In a true emergency, such as a hurricane or tornado, having more cash, potentially hundreds or even a few thousand dollars, could be critical for surviving until some normalcy returns, but that is a fairly big responsibility and far more than most families can just keep laying around. Plus, cash on hand is a clear target for thieves.

Everyday Needs

It is smart to have a few weeks, even months, of basic, every day necessities on hand. These can be used in an emergency such as a natural disaster or seasonal bad weather (local flooding or a snow storm), but they are another form of financial preparedness in case of a financial downturn, such as a job loss. This should include not just food but any item you need every day. These basics include soap (dish, clothing, and body), sanitary napkins, toilet paper, batteries, and other relatively small (and individually inexpensive) items. For long-term storage, most items need to be somewhere cool, dry, and safe from critters, and they need to be rotated. This is fairly obvious for food, but mice will happily chew up your toilet paper for their nests and batteries go bad, so it is important to use the oldest ones first.

In addition to climate control, food also needs to be prepared for long-term storage. A cardboard box is neither prepared for long term storage nor safe from critters. There are tons of books, videos, even entire websites on long-term food storage but it boils down to preparing it (canning or dehydrating for most foods), storing it (generally Mylar bags with oxygen absorbers for anything not canned), and maintaining safe conditions (low humidity and heat). Book 2 in this series is a cookbook that discusses long-term food storage

STORING AND HIDING ASSETS

Weapons and Ammo

Weapons must be secured. Firearms, in particular, should be locked up when not in use, preferably in a safe that can't be picked up and moved without heavy machinery. The very last thing most people want to have stolen is any firearm or other weapons they own. The thief is, by definition, a criminal and may well use their property to commit other crimes. Firearms regulations vary by state so check your state's requirements regarding storing firearms, ammunition, and other weapons carefully. Some states require additional ammo to be stored separately. Ammo boxes are perfect for storing, you guessed it, ammo.

Bow and arrows are also very popular, but the best way to store them depends on the kind of bow. A recurve bow needs to be stored unstrung, but compound bows are stored strung. Arrows go in a tube or quiver. No matter what the piece of equipment, it needs kept away from extreme temperatures (the attic) and high humidity (the basement).

Activity

With your parents' help, find a place to hide something of value to you. Make sure you can remember where it is and are able to get it back out.

Quick Quiz

T/F   Firearms and ammunition should always be stored together, legally speaking.

T/F   The best safe is one you can easily pick up and move.

T/F   There is no need to store extra for everyday items such as toilet paper and hand sanitizer.

T/F   It is important to have a small amount of cash on hand.

T/F   Social security cards, wills, passports/citizenship papers, marriage/divorce paperwork, and birth certificates are just a few of the important papers that should be kept in a safe place.

Resources

Articles

5 Common Places to Avoid Hiding Your Jewelry
retireby40.org/5-places-avoid-hiding-jewelry

15 Secret Hiding Places That Will Fool Even the Smartest Burgler
www.diyncrafts.com/3833/home/15-secret-hiding-places-will-fool-even-smartest-burglar

A Secret Place to Hide Jewelry
snappyliving.com/a-secret-place-to-hide-jewelry/

Hide Your Stuff In Plain Sight and a Burglar Will Be Baffled
www.patriotheadquarters.com/the-best-hiding-places-home

Books

101 Secret Hiding Places: Hide What You Don't Want Found (Survival Guide Series Book 1) by George Shepherd

The Official C.I.A. Manual of Trickery and Deception by H. Keith Melton and Robert Wallace

Other

Search for "fireproof document bags" and "fireproof safe".

{Nine}

Starting and Ending a Job

These may seem like opposites, but they aren't really. They are part of a continuum. For most people, one job leads to another, and another, and another, until they either retire or die. There will be starts and stops and changes along the way, most notably when you train for a new career path, move, or your company moves/closes/eliminates your job. Each of those creates choices and opportunities for you, some good, some bad.

Finishing high school and college are the most obvious examples of education but trade schools and certifications (including vo-tech) arguably actually offer a pathway to more fields with more openings than a lot of college degrees and most people get their first job before they graduate from high school.

Even with a college degree, many fields require more training, often called continuing education. After finishing law school, for example, you need to pass the bar exam in each state you plan to practice in, then do CLE (Continuing Legal Education) as long as you continue practicing law. Part of the CLE needs to be in your practice area but some can be in a new area you might want to start working in. That means that even after 19 years of education, a lawyer can educate themselves and change to a different career path within law.

One skill not covered in this chapter is negotiating a salary. Discussed in Chapter Seven, negotiating a salary is part of getting a job, normally the very last part before you actually start. Negotiating a severance package may be as well but probably not until you have decades of work experience. At the highest levels of corporations, portions of this are negotiated when executives are hired.

Getting a Job

For most people, parents or another relative or friend are key to securing their first job. Depending on age, they may need to drive you or provide you with a car to drive yourself. Friends, family, and who you know will always play an important part in finding a job but the longer you work, the more important your resume, experience, skills, and references become.

Resume

Resumes as a physical document are less important seemingly every day as more and more companies move to online application systems but employers still need the same information a paper resume contains. The basics are your contact information (name, address, phone number, email), education (certificates, major/minor/focus, degrees, year received), past jobs (company, job title, years worked, description), special skills, and any other important information. And it must all fit on one sheet of 8.5x11 paper in a normal, readable font size.

Most of the information is pretty straightforward. The parts that take thought and work are the job description, special skills, and "other." Use active verbs and list the most important parts of your job, especially ones that are relevant to the job you are applying for. If you worked as a bookseller and are applying to be a receptionist, focus on customer interaction in the description. If you are applying to be a file clerk, focus on shelving and organizing books. If you took the initiative to do a special project like starting a morning reading-to-

toddlers program that allowed moms to shop and resulted in an increase of X% in store sales, be sure to include that with any concrete, verifiable numbers you have.

Special Skills typically include computer programs you know, machines you can operate, and specialized training. If you know another language, include it here even if it doesn't seem related. One young man applied for a job as a computer programmer and included the entirely irrelevant fact that he spoke Russian. The hiring manager felt like all the resumes looked virtually identical–except for his knowledge of Russian. He got the job because of that, even though it wasn't required.

"Other" is a place to include outside activities that may be relevant and any awards that may impress. The Girl Scout Gold Award and Boy Scout Eagle are two that should always be included because they are hard to earn and show a certain moral fiber and ability to follow through that companies like, even decades later. It is a place to make yourself stand out, in a good way, particularly when you are starting out or starting over in a new field and don't have much job experience yet.

Interviewing

The next step is to interview for the job. This can range from a few minutes for an unskilled hourly job to multiple multi-hour interviews on different days for a high-level job. Most jobs are won or lost during the interview. Before you go, do some research to understand what the company does and, if possible, who you will be working for and with. This can be as simple as a Google search or a walk around the store looking at the merchandise.

No matter what the level, dressing nicely is expected. Wear nice, closed toed shoes, *not* sandals or flip-flops; a dressy blouse or button-down shirt; and a nice skirt or slacks. Be well-groomed, which means deodorant, a recent shower, neatly fixed and clean hair, light make-up, and minimal jewelry. Minimal jewelry means it can't be distracting. Look in the mirror and bob your head and shrug your shoulders. If your anything swings or glitters when you do that, it will probably be distracting and may not be the best choice. "Odd" or "extreme" jewelry such as nose rings, tongue rings, or any other jewelry that wouldn't have been worn on *Mad Men* should be left at home.

After the interview, it is a good idea to send a thank you note. An emailed thank you note is acceptable in many circumstances but a hand-written paper one is rarer and will have more of an impact. Sometimes, a thank you note makes the difference between getting a job and not getting it. Thank you notes are discussed more in Chapter Ten.

References

For your first job, teachers, family, youth group leaders, and close family friends will be about your only choices for references. Everyone knows and accepts this. After that point, most companies will be contacting your previous employers to see how you performed as an employee. If you had a manager and an assistant manager and the assistant knew you better or worked with you more, or you have another reason to think they might be a better reference, it's perfectly OK to list them instead but know that your potential new employer may call and talk to the manager as well.

It's a good idea to keep in touch with a few people you can use as references, so you have current contact information if you need to use them as references in the future. Most companies will want around three references. If you have four or five, then you are covered even if one or two are unavailable when you need a reference.

The Offer and Negotiating the Details

When they decide to offer you a job, the hiring manager will probably call and discuss some details with you such as the job title, work location, salary (amount, hourly or annual, and if you will receive overtime), start date, hours per week, and any benefits you may receive, such as a corporate discount. Some of these items may be negotiable, such as your start date; others will not be, such as corporate discounts. (Negotiating a salary is discussed in Chapter Seven.) Really, for most first jobs the only part that is negotiated is the start date and that is usually fast and easy.

For your start date, there will always be a date they really need you to start by or they will find someone different but bosses are people too. If your family vacation is scheduled for June 20-25 and they want you to start the 21st, just let them know and most will be perfectly happy to have you start the 26th instead. Of course, if you are flat broke and want to start sooner, you can tell them that too and they might be able to have you start sooner, although it does take a certain amount of time for the hiring paperwork to be processed.

Once you agree on the basic terms, all but the smallest companies will write an offer letter and mail or email it to you. The offer letter will probably include a list of items to bring your first day, specifically including your original social security card. Make sure you have them so you can finish all the legally required paperwork and become a paid employee of your new company.

Leaving Your Job

This can be voluntary, or not. It can be on good terms, or not. It's important to keep in mind that someone can leave voluntarily but on bad terms or involuntarily but on good terms. It depends in large part on how you conduct yourself both as an employee and on your way out, and it has a major impact on how good your reference from the company will be.

Companies, especially big companies, limit how much and what managers can say about a former employee when they give references, particularly if it is negative, to avoid possible lawsuits but other employers are fully aware of that. They take into account details like whether your reference/former boss sounds like talking about you brings up pleasant memories or something more akin to being sprayed by a skunk.

Losing a job involuntarily happens to everyone eventually, some more unexpectedly than others. Companies go out of business, downsize, lay off, and otherwise eliminate jobs. Some are seasonal or short-term to begin with and have a known end date. Other times, someone just isn't in the right job for them or is fired for doing a lousy job. While a lot of people are fired or lose a job because they screwed up or didn't do a very good job, many others did nothing wrong. When it happens to you, your first priority will probably be getting a new job but you do need to think about why you lost your job at some point to ensure it doesn't happen again.

Conducting Yourself Well

The way you leave a job can impact your ability to get a new job because you will need references for other jobs, as already discussed. Most companies have a questionnaire of some sort for "separating" individuals. That means anyone who is leaving for any reason, including quitting and being fired. Be careful how you answer this. Your answers should be truthful but don't be mean or nasty. Don't whine and complain.

When You Don't Have Another Job Waiting

What next? Start looking for a new job and reduce your expenditures. Even if someone else pays most of your expenses, you should still cut back so they money you have lasts longer. It's better to do one or two small, fun things a week until you have a new job than to have one great week, then be stuck at home with no money until your first paycheck arrives.

The first and most obvious change most people need to make to reduce their expenses is eating out less, particularly lunch for anyone working full time, followed by all other expenses related to going out to clubs, movies, and other events. All discretionary (non-essential, just for fun) shopping stops. Check your bills and see what can be decreased, starting with your cell phone and any subscription services/recurring expenses/memberships you have.

Activity

Think of a company you would like to work for and research them as if you were going to interview for a job. If they have a branch near you, find out if there is a job you are qualified for. If so, apply.

Quick Quiz

T/F   Who you know is never important during a job search.

T/F   People only lose a job if they screw up.

T/F   Being prepared for a job interview is important.

T/F   Once you decide to leave a job, how you act doesn't matter.

T/F   Once you are lose one job, it is impossible to get another one.

Resources

Articles

Best (and Worst) Reasons for Leaving a Job
www.thebalancecareers.com/reasons-for-leaving-a-job-2061664

How Teens Can Get That First Job
middleearthnj.wordpress.com/2011/03/07/how-teens-can-get-that-first-job/

How to Handle Leaving Your Job
www.thebalancecareers.com/how-to-handle-leaving-your-job-2062294

Job Application Tips for Teenagers
www.thebalancecareers.com/job-application-tips-for-teenagers-2061581

Job Interview Thank You Notes
www.job-hunt.org/job_interviews/sample-interview-thank-you-notes.shtml

Part-Time Job Resume Example for a Teen
www.thebalancecareers.com/part-time-job-resume-example-for-a-teen-2063248

Quitting a Job
www.monster.com/career-advice/workplace/quitting-job

Resume Examples for Teens: Templates, Builder & Writing Guide [+Tips]
zety.com/blog/teen-resume-example

The Right (and Wrong) Way to Ask Someone to be a Reference
middleearthnj.wordpress.com/2011/03/07/how-teens-can-get-that-first-job/

Books

Hey, Get a Job! A Teen Guide for Getting and Keeping a Job by Jennie Withers

Introverts: Leverage Your Strengths for an Effective Job Search by Gabrielea Casineau

Out-of-Work to Making Money by Anne Emerick

Survival Guide to Interviews by Rebekah Sack

Ultimate Garage Sales: Your Guides to Having a Hugely Successful and Highly Profitable Garage Sale! By Gregory Quintile

*Women Don't Ask: The High Cost of Avoiding Negotiation and Positive Strategies for Change by Linda Babcock and Sara Laschever

Scouting-Specific

Comparison Shopping Badge (6th-8th Graders)
forgirls.girlscouts.org/home/badgeexplorer/#comparison-shopping

Videos

8 Smart Questions to Ask Hiring Managers in a Job Interview
www.youtube.com/watch?v=Y95eI-ek_E8

Job Interview Tips for Teens
www.youtube.com/watch?v=88Mwb2bnOMk

No work experience? Why should we hire you? Teen job interviews with no work experience (part 1)
www.youtube.com/watch?v=UeOIb6s0pVM

What to Expect in a Fast Food Interview |_Fast Food Interview Questions
www.youtube.com/watch?v=SWfGlYVQt8c

{TEN}

MANNERS

Working with others is part of life. Just because you've been doing it since preschool doesn't mean you are good at it, nor does it mean you know some of the skills that are important in the adult world that the school world glosses over, even if you are already working in the adult world.

Shaking Hands and Greeting

Shaking hands is a normal greeting in most Western cultures. There will be times that you must shake hands with people that you would rather not touch, whether you are a kid or an adult. It happens, accept it. This is one time when you really do need to accept touching someone you really might not want to touch, but it is OK to keep it to a literal second. Anything over three or four seconds will usually seem overly long in any event.

The older you get, the more important this skill becomes. During interviews, including college, scholarship, and job interviews, the interviewer will almost certainly make some judgments based on your handshake. Depending on the situation, you may be given a name tag. If you put it on the right side of your chest, the eyes of the person shaking your hand will automatically go to your name tag. It's not necessary, most people won't even notice, but it is a nice gesture.

People often introduce themselves while shaking hands. A simple introduction ("Hi, I'm Bethanne" or "Hi, I'm Bethanne Kim") is usually enough and the handshake should continue while both people introduce themselves. Whether the other person gives their first name or first and last, you should do the same. If they introduce themselves as Mrs./Mr./Dr./General Washington, then you should give them your first and last name. If you aren't sure, introduce yourself this way. ("Hi, I'm Bethanne Kim.") If they just give their first name ("Hi, I'm George"), you it's safe for you to do the same ("Hi, I'm Bethanne"). They will decide what to call you from that. As an adult, respond using Mrs./Mr./Dr./General YourLastName. ("Hi, I'm Mrs. Kim.")

Make sure to stand and look the other person in the eyes when you greet them and shake their hand. Don't look at the ground, whatever is behind them, their chest, or anything else. If looking them in the eyes *really* makes you uncomfortable, try looking at their ear or their nose. It is close enough to make it look like you are looking them in the eye.

Proper Technique

Extend your right hand and grip the other person's right hand with it. Move your hands up and down in the air, generally three times or so is enough, then release your grip on their hand and your hand can drop back to your side.

With proper grip, no one's hands are being deformed by excessive pressure and both hands are held together firmly enough that a slight (but not huge) tug would be needed to pull out before both parties released the handshake.

What to Avoid

The two biggest problems with handshakes are the limp-fish handshake and the bone-crusher. The limp-fish is when so little pressure is exerted that the limp-fish person's hand would literally slide out if they stopped supporting the weight of their arm. This makes the person look weak.

The bone-crusher is when it feels like the person on the receiving end couldn't wrench their arm out of the handshake if they put their full body weight into it. Not surprisingly, it tends to feel like the hand bones are being crushed. This makes a person seem either overly aggressive or as if they are over-compensating for being afraid.

Apologizing

Losing your temper and saying or doing something you shouldn't is very easy, especially when you are upset. It happens to everyone at some point and sometimes leads to needing to apologize, a skill many people never learn. Apologizing is difficult because a genuine apology involves accepting that you did or said something wrong, and that can be hard to do.

A Proper Apology

A real apology includes saying you are sorry, what you did wrong or didn't do that you should have, and that you won't do it again. Bonus points for acknowledging the other persons feelings. Also, when spoken by not-sorry people with an attitude, the word "sorry" has anywhere from three to eighty-seven or more syllables, not the actual two syllables. Do not be that attitudinal person. It will not improve the situation.

> *No:* Soorrreeee your Lego set got smashed. It was stupid anyhow. [This doesn't acknowledge you did anything wrong, much less actually say you were sorry.]

> *Yes:* I'm sorry I broke your Lego set. I won't run in the living room next time.

> *Bonus:* I'm sorry I broke you're the Lego set you just finished. I shouldn't have been running in the living room. I know you worked really hard on it.

Look the person in the eye while you apologize and don't giggle or grin like the whole thing is really funny to you.

Choosing Not to Apologize

There are times in life when it is better not to apologize, but it takes a fair amount of life experience to understand when those are, and it is usually better to err on the side of apologizing when you may not need to than not apologizing when you may need to. (In other words, if in doubt, apologize.) The most important times this is true involve legal issues where you may end up accidentally, for example, admitting to being at-fault in a traffic accident, even if you weren't the one at fault, by apologizing. The more common examples are things like standing up for your beliefs, even if they upset someone else and experiencing your own emotions (how you act our based on those is a different matter).

If you have a person who is easily offended and expects an apology for every little thing but never (or rarely) apologizes themselves, you will probably reach a point when you don't want to apologize to them no matter what happens. That is a choice you will have to make for yourself, but know that it may permanently damage your relationship. Also know that you can simply give a short "I'm sorry" instead of a more complete apology. You may also choose to grit your teeth and apologize for the sake so others around that person don't have to put up with them being in a bad mood.

Thank You Notes

It may seem unimportant, like a minor detail or after-thought, but thank you notes are an important way to show someone you appreciate their time, effort, or thoughtfulness. Many people only send thank you notes for their wedding (and possibly baby) gifts, but you really should send them for your birthday, graduation, and any other time you receive a gift. Parents and close family members won't expect them, but will be pleasantly surprised if you give them a note.

In the past, perfect penmanship and poetic prose may have been expected, but those days are long gone. Most of us type far more than we handwrite, and handwritten things can't be edited and rewritten. Most recipients will be understanding of less-than-perfect handwriting. Do your best and make sure it looks neat. The closer you are to adulthood, the higher the expectation for it to be generally well-written and free of obvious spelling errors. Perfect is a bonus, not an expectation.

If you want to go the extra mile, you can buy high quality writing paper/cards and envelopes, and fountain pens and ink. Personally, I love fountain pens because I can buy any color ink I want. I'm not limited to a few colors! Plus, since I use a refillable bladder, a single recyclable glass bottle can last for years. There are also disposable fountain pens, which are a nice way to try them.

Thank you notes are important to send anyone who interviews or helps you when you are trying to get a job. They can make the difference between getting a job offer and not getting one. For most things, you need to send a note within one month, but it should ideally be within a day or two after a job interview.

These are most often short notes, written on small cards. Once you get the hang of it, they are easy to do. Start with a salutation ("Dear Mrs. Lee"), then actually say thank you. That means literally write the words "thank you" at the beginning of the note, then personalize it with some details about the gift and how you plan to use it, especially if it was a gift of money. Tell them you look forward to seeing them (if you will), thank them a second time, then close with a final thank you and either "Sincerely," or "Love," followed by your signature.

Since you may be wondering, yes, you can email a thank-you note, but a physical, paper note makes more of an impression.

MANNERS

Disappointing Others

It is inevitable that eventually you will do (or not do) something and disappoint a person who matters to you, including your boss. I really want to say never do the thing that disappointed the other person again, but the reality is that their expectations may be wrong, or they may not be good people for you. You need to know what is right and wrong, and what matters to you. If a friend, family member, co-worker, or boss is disappointed in you because you didn't help them cover up theft, you are right and they are wrong. Get out of that environment as fast as you can.

Assuming that's not the case, apologize if it's appropriate, even if you don't think it was a big deal, then try to make it better. Remember that you can't change other people's emotions and it's easy to misread them, especially for people you don't know well. "Hangry" is a prime example.

Your action may seem small an unimportant to you, but be a big deal to them, or the other way around. My father spoiled a Mother's Day breakfast surprise my son had planned by talking about exactly what he was going to make in front of me and my mom. It never even occurred to my Dad that it might be a big deal, but my son had been planning to surprise us and was quite excited, so this was a huge disappointment for my little guy. A genuine apology from Grampa would've meant the world to him and cost his Grampa nothing.

Activity

Practice shaking hands and greeting someone new.

Quick Quiz

T/F   If you nearly break a bone when you shake someone's hand, it shows that you are a strong leader.

T/F   Never apologize. It shows weakness.

T/F   Disappointing others is part of life.

T/F   Look people in the eye when you shake their hand.

T/F   Sometimes you have to apologize even though you didn't do
      anything wrong.

Resources

Articles

20 Things You Don't Have to Apologize For
tinybuddha.com/blog/20-things-you-dont-have-to-apologize-for/

The 8 Best Fountain Ink Pens of 2019
www.thebalancesmb.com/best-fountain-ink-pens-4155876/

Choosing the Best Disposable Fountain Pen
fountainpenlove.com/fountain-pen-reviews/choosing-the-best-disposable-
fountain-pen/

Does and Don'ts of Unforgettable Thank You Notes
www.thespruce.com/how-to-write-thank-you-letters-1196798

How NOT to Apologize
www.liveabout.com/how-not-to-apologize-1385228

How To Write a Charming Thank You Note
www.southernliving.com/home-garden/solutions/thank-you-note

How to Write a Thank You Note*
ideas.hallmark.com/articles/thank-you-ideas/how-to-write-a-thank-you-note/

Thoughtful Wording For A Thank You Note
www.thespruce.com/thoughtful-wording-thank-you-note-1216778

When You Should Not Apologize
www.liveabout.com/when-you-should-not-apologize-1384855

Writing Paper
www.quotesandsayings.com/general/writing-paper/

Books

101 Ways to Say Thank You: Notes of Gratitude for All Occasions by Kelly Browne

How to Write Heartfelt Letters to Treasure by Lynette M. Smith

Why Won't You Apologize?: Healing Big Betrayals and Everyday Hurts by Harriet Lerner

Other

Pilot Varsity Disposable Fountain Pen

Thank You Notes (customizable options available online)

Videos

How to Apologize
www.youtube.com/watch?v=z3H_GgtE3Tc

How to Apologize (A Guide for People Who Suck At It)
www.youtube.com/watch?v=EdinmmFxTuI

How to Shake Hands & Introduce Yourself | Good Manners
www.youtube.com/watch?v=41BdlgNyKFI

{PART 3}
CYBER AND PERSONAL SECURITY

Schools usually talk about cyber-safety to some degree, but they don't necessarily talk about what dangers are online, other than being hacked and online stranger danger. They also don't talk about how things change as you grow up and do more online.

Personal Information: Do you know what is considered personal information and how to keep it safe? Setting good passwords and keeping them safe is part of keeping your personal information safe. Knowing when to give your real information, how much to give, and when not to give it is another important element.

Danger at Home: Fire safety and fire escape plans are discussed regularly in elementary schools, but fires aren't the only possible danger in your home.

Online Safety: One of the most common pieces of advice has been to "never meet someone you met online in real life." That's probably good advice in elementary school, but it doesn't hold up into adulthood where many people use online dating services and make friends in online forums. Knowing the rules of safe online interaction, and when and how it is safe to break them, is very important.

Meeting Strangers: Most strangers are perfectly harmless, but some are very, very dangerous. Being able to spot the warning signs of those dangerous strangers can be the difference between being safe, and not. So can being cautious and safe even with those strangers who seem 100% safe.

{ELEVEN}

PERSONAL INFORMATION

Your name, birthday, social security number, address, phone number, and mother's maiden name (her last name before she was married) are all considered "personal information." If someone has that information, it makes "identity theft" easier. Why is your mom's maiden name included? Banks and other financial institutions often use this as a security question. They also often ask the name of your first pet and the town you grew up in. You may *think* you don't have anything to steal now, but if you are a legal US citizen, you have a Social Security Number and people can do very bad things to your financial future with just that number.

A paper shredder is your friend. A cross-cut confetti shredder is your BFF. Remember to treat your shredder friends kindly–empty them, oil them, and do any other maintenance they need, with adult help if needed.

Identity Theft

Through most of human history, your identity was who you are as a person, full stop. Most of the time, there was no paper, electronic, or other part to it. Over time, as the population grew it became harder and harder to keep track of people. More and more people had the same names, which was confusing. People started being assigned numbers to keep track of them. The military did this fairly early. Drivers licenses were another place people started having numbers issued to identify them instead of just their own person. In the 1930s, Social Security was introduced in the USA and people received Social Security Numbers. Banks started using numbers to identify their customers just as the banks themselves are identified by numbers.

Military ID, Social Security, and bank numbers are all associated with people receiving money, eventually or immediately. Drivers Licenses are one of the few forms of photo ID that can be used to prove a person is who they say they are. People who don't drive can be issued a State ID, which has the same information and identification functions, it just doesn't allow them to drive. These are most common among the elderly who no longer drive and in big cities with great mass transit where people don't need to drive.

Our lives are contained in data banks, numbered accounts, numbered files, and electronic records. A person's face and mind cannot be stolen. Those other things can be stolen or a bad person can convince the electronic gatekeepers that they are the legitimate owner of them. That is Identity Theft. Someone steals enough of your real information to fake being you. They generally use that to steal your money or get credit in your name that they never pay back, leaving you with the bill.

Guard your personal information, and guard it well.

An Online Persona

The easiest way to avoid sharing personal information online is to have an online persona. That's a nice way of saying **"lie about key bits of information to stay safe."** This isn't saying "lie about everything" but other kids (and their parents) will understand if you use a pretend name, fake birthday, and different town.

It isn't OK to use a birthday that is very different from your real one. There are good reasons websites need to have your birthday, as a kid, to make certain that you aren't going on websites that are inappropriate for your age. That doesn't mean you can't use one that's off by a little bit. Just don't say you're 15 when you're 11.

If your birthday is May 27, 2087 (side note: it's super cool that you traveled back in time!) and you use December 15, 2086, it's close enough that you shouldn't run into anything really inappropriate on a website. It also shouldn't freak out people you meet online but later meet in real life, especially if you explain that it's just part of staying safe online.

With the exception of bank websites, I have entered a fake birthday every time I needed to enter my birthday since I started going online. It is extremely consistent. It is also a different month, date, and year from my real birthday, but it's not off by very much. Just enough to make identity theft more difficult. I have used this so many places for so many years that it almost feels like it really is my (second) birthday! My son even bakes me a cake some years, although I think that's more about him wanting cake.

Passwords

Passwords and pin numbers have become a regular, normal part of life. It's not unusual for toddlers and preschoolers to have passwords (admittedly used by adults) for apps and online games. As a parent, I have eleven different passwords just for email accounts! Of course that includes my kids' accounts because we need to be able to see their email accounts. (And yes, I know they can easily set up accounts we don't know about, but that is a different issue.) In total, I could have 100 different accounts that require passwords.

Yikes! How to keep track of it all?!? For one thing, many of those are throw-away sites. I had to "establish an account" to read an article or buy a single item. I didn't let them store any form of payment data, and I didn't use all (or any) of my real information, making it far less useful for identity theft.

Good Passwords

Because longer passwords are harder to break, pass phrases are a good idea. Breaking "petcat1" wouldn't take very long. Breaking "My cat Sheba loves mice!" will take *much* longer and probably isn't much harder for you to remember. Today, a lot of sites have a "strength indicator" that tells you if a password is weak, average, or strong. A strong password is longer (preferably 13 characters), and contains a mix of upper and lower case letters, numbers, and symbols. Many sites won't let you set a password unless it is a certain length and at least "average" strength.

It goes against the common wisdom, but my throw-away accounts just do not matter so I use the same two passwords for most of them. And neither does the separate email account I use just for these accounts, including blogs and news sites. Since all the email updates go there, my "personal" account stays fairly empty and it's easy to find emails.

I have one password for easily 20-30 websites that I just don't care about. Frankly, there is *no* information saved on those sites and I stand to lose nothing if my accounts are hacked. The simplicity of a single, easily-remembered password is worth the miniscule risk attached to doing this. (For some of these sites, I will probably literally never visit them again.)

Security

Setting up passwords and keeping track of them can be a huge pain, especially if you don't know how to create a *good* password. It's also important to have different passwords for different sites. Websites and email accounts can be hacked and passwords stolen. Because of that, each account should have a unique password.

Once you set up good passwords, keeping them safe is important. Once you have more than four or five passwords, it is virtually impossible to remember them all. That leaves you with a choice: keep track of them electronically or on paper. Either way, keep the list safe.

Writing them down on paper or keeping them electronically are the two basic choices. Either way, keep the information secure. Online, password protect the document. On paper, keep it securely hidden away, possibly locked in a drawer, but not next to your computer.

It is also good to not fully write out the information. I can safely abbreviate one email address l@ because I only have one email with that name. I know what comes after the @ but a thief probably wouldn't. If I write [MomAddress][1stBank], I know what those things are but a would-be thief almost certainly doesn't.

Activity

Create an email, Kindle, or other account with your parent's help. Be sure the password is secure and decide, with their help, how much of your real name and information to use.

OR

Create a modified profile that you can use regularly online. Choose a birthday that is close to your real birthday, but with different day, month and year. The year has to be close to your real birthday because there are very strong rules about how old you have to be to do certain things online.

With your parents, decide what to list as your town. If there is a big city near you, that may be a good choice. Choose somewhere that is generally near you, but not close enough that an online stranger can find you.

Quick Quiz

T/F   You must always use your real name, birthday, and other information online.

T/F   Identity theft creates huge problems.

T/F   "password" is a stronger password than "Nittany Lions 2025 rule!!"

T/F   It's never OK to reuse a password or user name.

T/F   Today, much of our lives and key data is contained in data files that can be hacked.

Resources

Articles

How to Wean Yourself Off Smartphones and Social Media
www.pcmag.com/feature/360420/how-to-wean-yourself-off-smartphones-and-social-media

Identity Theft
www.usa.gov/identity-theft

Ten Tips to Prevent Identity Theft
www.lifewire.com/ten-tips-to-prevent-identity-theft-2487430

Books

Password Log Book

Your Identity Theft Protection Game Plan by Damian Brindle

Scouting-Specific

Cyber Chip
www.scouting.org/training/youth-protection/cyber-chip/

Crime Prevention Merit Badge
meritbadge.org/wiki/index.php/Crime_Prevention

{TWELVE}

DANGER AT HOME

Your home should feel like the safest place in your life, or at least one of them, but sometimes it doesn't. Sometimes there is an emergency in your own home. Can you handle these scenarios? The most important single aspect is to simply be prepared, to think through what you will do if confronted with a certain set of circumstances.

An Adult Needs 911

Pick up the phone and call 911 or whatever the local emergency number is. Call another adult to help, preferably someone who knows their medical history very well.

Fire

Schools cover this extensively, so you probably already know: Get out and call 911–*in that order*. Don't stop to rescue a pet. Do cover your nose and mouth with a cloth, better yet a wet cloth, to help keep smoke and ash out of your throat and lungs. Go to a pre-designated meeting place and wait for your family and the emergency first responders.

If it's a tiny fire that's just started, you can douse it with water BUT NEVER PUT WATER ON A GREASE FIRE, or cover it with a special fire-blanket designed to put out fires, if you have one. For a grease fire, smother it to starve it of oxygen. You can do this by covering the pot with a cookie tray, but make sure there aren't any openings to allow air in to continue feeding it. Covering it in baking soda is an alternative method.

Home Intruder/Home Invasion

You have a plan for a house fire. Do you have a plan for a home intruder or home invasion? Some elements are the same, such as deciding on a safe place a safe distance from the house to meet and having an escape plan. Unlike a fire, you also need a plan for a safe place to hide if you can't get out. (In a fire, that is pretty much a death trap because you want to be found and rescued.)

One simple tip to stay safe: Never open the door to a stranger. Not even a crack. If the police show up, you can call to confirm it is a real police officer before letting them in or opening the door, if you do let them in or open the door.

Grab your cell phone if you can, turn the ringer OFF, and hide or escape. If you can escape, get far enough from your house to feel safe before stopping. In a big city apartment, that may be the building lobby, another floor, or even the apartment next door. In a rural area, it may be a mile or two down the road. If you have to travel a distance, you can call for help while you keep moving. Otherwise, call when you are safe and tell the police what happened. You should also call and warn anyone else who might be headed to your home soon, like your parents, grandparents, siblings, or friends.

If you can't get out and are hidden in the house, call or text the police for help, but DO NOT text if there is any chance it will make noise when you receive a text back. Do not try to be a hero, especially if they are armed. If there is someone else in the home with you (friends or family), help them hide or escape. If you are hidden, escape if you get a very clear chance. If not, stay hidden until they leave. "Catching the bad guy" isn't the goal. Staying safe, and keeping those around you safe, is the goal. Many home invasions are robberies when the home owner is at home, with no intention of being violent. In short, if they don't feel like they are in danger, there is a good chance you won't be in danger either. If you aren't able to escape or hide, don't *ever* try pulling a weapon on an armed intruder unless you are, yourself a highly trained professional. Don't be aggressive. Remain calm, even though it may seem impossible.

Remember: Stay quiet! It could be your life on the line if you don't.

Police at the Door

If the police are at your door, you are not required to let them in unless they have a warrant or you are on parole/probation. Being belligerent or angry in dealing with them would, however, be an extremely poor choice, and one that can easily end up with you in jail even if you have otherwise done nothing wrong. Videotaping the encounter, even if you don't open the door, is a good idea for your protection and the officer's.

You can call local police dispatch to confirm that they are real police officers, not criminals pretending to be cops to attack you more easily, before answering. If your parents are home, call them to the door or find them and ask them what to do. The police may simply be asking for information about a person they are trying to find, like a robber who may have fled in the area. If so, tell them if you know anything. If not, tell them that so they can continue the search with as much information as possible.

The other common reason is that there was a noise complaint against you. If so, simply apologize, turn down the noise, and keep it turned down–even if you think it was already quiet enough. Avoid ever being so loud that you can't hear a knock at the door or the doorbell.

To be very, very clear: Most police are good people trying to protect people in their jurisdiction, but not all are. Even among those who are good people, they can do things with the best of intentions that have bad consequences. Ask your parents if they are OK with you allowing police into your home, or even opening the door so they can see inside. If they aren't, ask them what you should do. In my house, if I see someone I don't know come up the walkway and knock on the front door, I sometimes walk out the back door and greet them from the driveway. That lets me talk to them with no danger of them forcing their way into my home. Because I'm in the driveway, I can run to the street, to a neighbors, or get in the car and drive away if they scare me.

Police are not legally allowed to enter without your permission, and inviting them inside gives them permission. If they simply need a few questions answered, you can easily do this through a closed or cracked open door. We have had officers and FBI at our home before and I would be very suspicious of any law enforcement officer who tried to force their way in. (The FBI was checking on a neighbor getting a security clearance, which is a normal occurrence in our area.) Most have stood several feet away from the door in a deliberately non-threatening manner.

Trapped

Snowstorms, floods, tornadoes, downed power lines–all sorts of things can leave people stuck in their home for a few days. Does your family have an emergency stash of food and supplies? Do you know where it is and how to access it? You should. If you don't, build one. It should include enough food, water, and basic sanitary supplies (toilet paper, hand sanitizer, soap) to last for at least two weeks, just to be safe. And, if you're honest, that two week supply can come in handy with just a bad virus running rampant through your family.

Activity

Make and practice an emergency plan for your entire family. Include variations for fire, home invasion, and being trapped. Also include a plan for how to respond if the police are at your door.

Quick Quiz

T/F   If anything at all goes wrong, call 911.

T/F   Fire drills and fire extinguishers save lives.

T/F   Emergency plans are a waste of time.

T/F   Never, ever–EVER–douse a grease fire with water.

T/F   Don't open the door for strangers.

Resources

Articles

Home invasion family survival tips
www.crimedoctor.com/home2.htm

How to Keep Safe During a House Fire
www.wikihow.com/Keep-Safe-During-a-House-Fire

How to stay safe during a home invasion.
nightlock.com/how-to-stay-safe-during-a-home-invasion/

Police at my door: What should I do?
www.flexyourrights.org/faqs/police-at-my-door-what-should-i-do/

Staying Safe at Home
www.baptistjax.com/health-library/caresheets/staying-safe-at-home

What to do if you are stopped by a police officer.
www.baltimorecountymd.gov/Agencies/police/community/stop2.html

Books

Secrets to Safety: Home Invasion Protection and Personal Defense by Alvin "Goldie" Mack, PhD

What to Expect When Calling 911: The Everyday Person's Guide to Calling 911 by C.R. Hartwell

Scouting-Specific

Crime Prevention Merit Badge
meritbadge.org/wiki/index.php/Crime_Prevention

Fire Safety Merit Badge
meritbadge.org/wiki/index.php/Fire_Safety

Safety Merit Badge
meritbadge.org/wiki/index.php/Safety

Videos

How to Survive a Home Invasion*
www.youtube.com/watch?v=Ixcqvk5oCrU

Deadliest Places You Could Be in a Home Invasion
www.youtube.com/watch?v=J0evmdEAFJI

Five Simple Steps to Survive A Home Invasion
www.youtube.com/watch?v=x7Chfzd7Cbc

{Thirteen}

Online Safety

Online safety is routinely covered in school, Scouts, and all kinds of other places, but it's a big subject. Ten years ago, people had only been online in large numbers for perhaps ten years, and not many had been online for that long. Today, many people spend a lot of time online and many more are digital natives. Making friends and dating people we meet online has become normal. Our comfort level, awareness of danger, and ways of handling online/offline interactions have changed a lot as they have become more and more a part of life.

Forums

Chat forums exist for every possible interest. They are one of the easiest places to meet strangers, one of the easiest places to overshare personal details, and somewhere it's easy to get conned into believing people are someone they aren't. In other words, you are an easy mark in online forums. Tread very carefully.

There will be times when you join a forum related to an extracurricular activity, such as robotics or cheerleading. You may "meet" someone in a thread who is going to be at an event you will be attending. They may genuinely be another person around your age and meeting up with them could be great, but they may be a predator.

Before you give them any information that will help them find you, talk to you parents and/or coach, read the section below on "Meeting in Real Life", then talk to your parents or coach again.

With that said, forums can be a great place to meet people with similar interests or problems to you. I know nearly four dozen women that I first "met" in an online forum for new moms nearly twenty years ago. I have only ever met a few in person. Within the group, there are some very strong bonds of friendship. We have been through losing children, parents, spouses, jobs, and pets; mental health problems; natural disasters; and every other major life change. These friendships are valuable to all of us.

Forums based on similar interests make it a lot easier to find answers to specialized questions and are quite simply *fun!* The problem is that in the course of posting and answering questions, it is easy to include details that can be used to learn a lot (too much) about you, and that's great for predators. Be cautious about how much you include, and remember that you can go back and delete comments.

Social Media

Chat forums are technically social media, but the term "social media" usually means sites and apps where people gather to be social and share personal information and photos. At the moment, these include Facebook, Instagram, Twitter, and SnapChat.

You have undoubtedly heard it before, but things can last forever on the internet. Despite that, it is possible to delete comments, posts, and other things you share online. There is nothing you can do about back-ups stored in data centers somewhere or things others have shared, downloaded, or screen grabbed, but the sooner you delete them, the fewer potential copies there are. Deleting old posts and comments is something you should do regularly.

Even more than chat forums, it is easy to let down your guard and share too much information for your safety. It's easy to leave little breadcrumbs of information all over your social media that, taken together, give predators a lot of detail about your life. You really should go back regularly (monthly, weekly, quarterly—whatever works for you) and delete comments and posts that reveal details about your personal life. This doesn't mean delete everything you've done, just items that may reveal too much, whether that is emotionally, socially, geographically (places you like to hang out, your schedule, etc.), or physically (especially in pictures). You should also delete anything that would look bad to a potential employer or college because they do look at social media, as you certainly know.

To give an example of how small things can add up, I got creeped out by a friend of a friend whose comments were starting to feel threatening. Before blocking him, I wanted to make sure he didn't live near me. In his posts, I found several that were to a small newspaper near Brooklyn. He had liked several NYC area politicians and restaurants, and a Brooklyn politician. Taken all together, it seemed clear that he lived in Brooklyn not anywhere near me, even though he never marked anything about where he lived. Could that be wrong? Certainly, but those are the kind of breadcrumbs we all leave and that a predator can use to find their target.

In addition, it's a good idea to titles instead of names for your closest family and friends. In over a decade on social media, my family still consists of Husband, Eldest, and Youngest in my posts. In addition to not providing names a predator could use, these help preserve my kids' privacy. Clearly, there are limits to this, but it's easy to do with a few people.

In short, be careful of what you share and delete old comments, posts, and images regularly. The chances of anyone going back to look at anything you posted more than a week or two ago are really fairly slim, so it's unlikely anyone will even notice. Predators, on the other hand, may comb through their intended victims information with a fine-tooth comb, looking for any bits of data they can use.

The book *It's Complicated* is written for adults who are nervous about kids online safety to help them understand how social media actually impacts kids, and that it's far from all bad.

Meeting Virtual Friends in Real Life

School will tell you to never, ever do this, and it's not bad advice–to a point. Eventually, you will make friends online and may want to meet in person, although it may not happen until you are an adult for practical reasons. It can be hard to remember, but the internet isn't that old. A lot of people date and even marry people they meet online, but it's barely been twenty years since online dating really started. Adults (especially ones who never did online dating and have few or no online friends) can see the dangers for kids in meeting people online, but they don't always see the benefits of being able to find people who share similar interests when there aren't any who live near you

As you grow up, groups of online friends (like my mommy friends mentioned earlier) will probably be your normal. The internet is a great place to find people who share your interests if you can't find anyone who live near you in real life. When your parents, teachers, and other adults fuss, remember that this really is still new and everyone is trying to work out the safety guidelines around meeting total strangers who may already know a lot about you. One hundred years is an eye-blink in the history of the human race. A mere hundred years ago, most people knew everyone in their town and women had just received the right to vote. Knowing how to stay safe, and keep those you love safe, when you could "meet" hundreds or even thousands of strangers in mere minutes by uploading a video or blog post can be hard.

My group's meet-up illustrates the number one thing to remember about meeting virtual friends in real life: Never, ever, EVER meet them anywhere except a reasonably busy public place in broad daylight (in our case, the zoo), and don't go alone. Bring an adult along. Depending on the situation, meeting in a group can be a good idea. Since an adult will be going with you, they can tell you if a group seems like a good idea or one-on-one sounds better. If you are an adult, then you need to make sure someone else knows who you are meeting, and where and why. Do not ever give people you only know online your home information, including details like your school or where your extra-curricular activities meet.

Webcams

Webcams can be hacked fairly easily. There are stories about people who leave their laptops open in their bedrooms and strangers are able to see them walking around naked by turning on the webcam the owner thought was safely turned off. Something as simple as part of a Post-it note® over the camera lens stops that. One really good way to cover a webcam is with electrical tape. It is black and completely opaque. It also only sticks to itself. If you cut a small piece and cover the webcam with it, the tape will cover it and no images will get through. The truly lovely thing about it is that it can easily be removed and put back because it doesn't leave a sticky residue. When you need to use the webcam, just uncover and use it. When you finish, remember to re-cover the camera.

Fake News

"Fake news" isn't just about big headlines splashed across all the major mainstream media sites. Fake news can be gossip about classmates or neighbors. It can be rumors about a business or family. No matter how big or small the target, it's always best to check if it's true or exaggerated. Most fake news has some element of truth to it but sometimes that's like saying a donut is wheat. Most (not all) donuts contain flour made out of wheat, but a donut is definitely not wheat.

Fake news hurts us all. Every time all the big media outlets post a sensational headline without fact-checking it first, it damages their collective reputations for being honest and trustworthy. Every time a person posts, shares, or tells a story or headline that is wrong, it hurts their credibility. Think about your friends. Are there some who often share stories that turn out to be wrong? Are there others who usually have done research enough to point out fake news? Whose opinion do you value more?

If a headline or story is shocking, take a minute to step back and look at it. Does it fit a pattern of previously known events? Is it probable? Is there another explanation? Occam's Razor is a problem-solving salutation that says the simplest solution is usually the right or best one. Apply this to fake news. Does the headline rely on a convoluted series of events or logic? Does it ignore recent well-known events or facts? Is it internally consistent? If a photo is from Florida, it shouldn't show icebergs. If it has a date stamp of 2011, then it can't be a current event.

Take a look at how quickly the story was published. When Notre Dame Cathedral went up in flames, of course the story was published immediately and updated frequently. That's not a surprise or a red flag for fake news. If a news outlet had come out with a culprit or explanation of how the fire started while it was still blazing out of control, that would have been a red flag that they were passing off conjecture (guesses) as facts.

Real journalism takes hard work, and that takes time. It also has facts to back it up, not simply opinions. Blue is better than red is 100% an opinion. Blue is better than red at calming people is a fact with science to back it up. Finding the studies that back up the second statement takes time and at least some skill to understand them and be confident that they are well-done, reputable studies.

Activity

Choose one of your social media accounts. Spend at least half an hour going through and deleting old posts and comments. Check your profile to make sure you aren't giving away too much personal information.

Quick Quiz

T/F It is important to be very careful when you meet an online "friend" in real life.

T/F Oversharing personal information on social media, including forums, is easy to do.

T/F Webcams can be accessed remotely, allowing people to watch you at any time if you haven't covered the camera.

T/F You should never delete old posts or comments.

T/F It is impossible to make a real friend online.

Resources

Articles

How to Disable Your Webcam (and Why You Should)
www.howtogeek.com/210921/how-to-disable-your-webcam-and-why-you-should/

Social Media, Pretend Friends, and the Lie of False Intimacy
www.convinceandconvert.com/social-media-tools/social-media-pretend-friends-and-the-lie-of-false-intimacy/

Spy Game: Dangers of Webcam Hacking and How to Avoid Them
www.avg.com/en/signal/how-hackers-can-hijack-your-webcam-to-spy-on-you

Books

The Bullying Workbook for Teens: Activities to Help You Deal with Social Aggression and Cyberbullying by Raychelle Cassada Lohmann and Julia V. Taylor

Fake News: Separating Truth from Fiction by Michael Miller

Fake News Nation: The Long History of Lies and Misinterpretations in America by James W. Cortada and William Aspray

Fighting Fake News: Teaching Critical Thinking and Media Literacy in a Digital Age by Brian C. Housand PhD

Follow Jesus: A Christian Teen's Guide to Navigating the Online World by Christine Carter

*It's Complicated; The Social Lives of Networked Teens by Danah Boyd

Social Media Investigation for Law Enforcement by Joshua Brunty and Katherine Helenek

Street Kids: The Lives of Runaway and Thrownaway Teens by R. Barri Flowers

*Teen Cyberbullying Investigated: Where Do Your Rights End and Consequences Begin? by Judge Tom Jacobs

The Truth Matters: A Citizen's Guide to Separating Facts from Lies and Stopping Fake News in its Tracks by Bruce Bartlett

Viral News on Social Media by Paul Lane

Scouting-Specific

Cyber Chip
www.scouting.org/Training/YouthProtection/CyberChip.aspx

Digital Technology Merit Badge
meritbadge.org/wiki/index.php/Digital_Technology

Netiquette Badge
forgirls.girlscouts.org/home/badgeexplorer/#netiquette

Videos

Mark Cuban: The Big Mistake You Don't Know You're Making on Social Media
www.inc.com/mark-cuban/playbook-biggest-mistake-social-media.html?cid=ps002playbook&sr_source=lift_facebook

*Truth or Fake2019: Four Tips for detecting fake news online
www.youtube.com/watch?v=EJDFeXomVvg

What is Fake News?
www.youtube.com/watch?v=FOZ0irgLwxU

"What one woman says is fake news is what another woman says is truth"
www.youtube.com/watch?v=7IKYFE4jp6s

{FOURTEEN}

MEETING STRANGERS

First, second, and third: <u>Most</u> strangers are not dangerous. A teeny, tiny portion of strangers are Bad People who will do Bad Things if they get the chance. Sadly, because those Bad Things can be So Very Bad, it is important to learn about how to recognize potential Stranger Danger and to be very careful around strangers. If something happens and you can't avoid a dangerous stranger, how do you handle that? Perhaps they followed you and trapped you, or perhaps you made a huge mistake and met them alone, whatever the reason, you need to find a way back to safety.

Since everyone has to meet new people (strangers) sometimes, this chapter discusses meeting new people politely first. If nothing else, there are new teachers every year, new kids in class, and new people in after-school activities. If you are in competitions, there are judges, referees, and other officials you need to interact with.

Meeting in Real Life (IRL)

When you are little, there are a lot of rules that adults give where you must "never" do X. As you grow up, that "never" gradually turns into "be careful when you" for a lot of things. Meeting people IRL that you know online is one of those things. In the past, people had "pen pals" for years and never, ever met. Pen pals wrote letters they mailed back and forth to each other. Some lived on opposite sides of the world. Online friends, including forum and online gaming friends, are a modern version of this.

As a little kid, it is unlikely that you will ever make a friend online that is such a good and unusual friend that you will both be able to convince you parents you should meet IRL, although it is possible. As you reach middle and high school, that can change. As an adult, it almost certainly will.

How Long Should You Wait?

Personally, I wouldn't meet anyone I had known online for less than six months to a year (minimum). Longer is *definitely* better.

What difference does the length of time make? If a Bad Person is online pretending to be someone different–a kid, a teen, a boy, a girl, a teacher, an expert in a field you are interested in, it doesn't matter– the odds are good that they will have the patience to wait for a few weeks or even a few months to con you out of something. Some may have the patience to wait for years, but odds are good that most will give up and go after easier prey. The longer you wait to meet, the less likely it is that they are pretending to be someone else.

A big part of the reason I am so comfortable with my online friends of nearly 20 years is that liars (including predators) simply couldn't keep track of their lies for that long. It's hard to keep lies straight and to remember them. The longer you interact, the harder it is to remember lies. Truthfully, I have known them for so long I straight up forget I have only known them online. When I visit one of these ladies, I feel as safe as I do with people I know IRL.

Why Meet?

How do you know if you "need" to meet them? Truthfully, in most cases, there is no need. You may *want* to meet, but that is different.

Online video chat should suffice to visit. In one case, I want to meet my friend because she is very ill and may die soon.

Every now and then, your online friend may have an interest in common that you can only work on together, in real life. Or one of you may be able to help the others with a problem. Sometimes, you have been friends for years and just want to hang out in person. Other times, it happens that one or both of you are taking a trip and will be unusually close to each other, making it possible to meet easily. In one case, an internet friend who lives near me had a piece of furniture to give me.

Whatever the reason, you both want to meet, think you need to meet, and have convinced your parents it is a good idea. What next?

Is it Safe?

How do you know it is safe to meet someone you "know" online? First, second, third, and foremost, they are someone you have known for months or years and they have been very, very consistent in what they tell you. The more you can find to confirm who they are, the better, but this is harder to do with kids.

As stated above, it's hard to keep track of lies. Everyone forgets some things, but if your online friend routinely forgets things they have told you happened or changes things about themselves, it's a bad sign. The more difference you spot between what they tell you different times, the worse a sign it is. Talk to your parents or another trusted adult but it's probably in your best interest to just move on. In rare cases, it may be a sign that your friend is in danger and needs help. DO NOT put yourself in danger to help them! Ask adults for help. Contact the police, child services, a school official, or another adult who can help and let you remain anonymous.

Fourth, don't meet alone. Make sure you have a trusted adult with you and expect them to bring a trusted adult too.

Where Should You Meet?

You probably guessed this, but in a public place, with your parents or another trusted adult with each of you. Be sure that others know when and where and who you will be meeting, just in case.

Do not let them convince you to go to another location that you need to drive to or where other people can't see you, such as taking a walk away from a crowded picnic area into a secluded wooded area. If you agreed to meet to see a movie and need to walk from a restaurant or coffee shop near the theater to the theater with your parents, that's OK, but don't let anyone pressure you into going somewhere that doesn't feel safe.

Dangerous Groups and Social Isolation

Any group (or person) that wants to separate you from your friends and family is almost certainly a danger to you–and that is true from the time you are a baby the whole way through extreme old age. This is true even if you know some, or most, of the people in the group, and it is true even if it is a family member. If you have learned to listen to your instincts (Chapter 1, *26 Basic Life Skills*), they will be a good guide as to whether a group is good for you or not.

Your family may try to separate you from your friends if they are a bad influence, but they won't be trying to take away **everyone** who loves and cares about you because your family loves and cares about you, even if it doesn't seem like it some days. There will almost certainly be friends from your past that they are happy to have you continue to hang out with, even if they think you have "fallen in with a bad crowd" recently.

Dangerous groups want to separate you from the people who truly know and care about you because those people will see that you are doing bad things and try to stop you. Sometimes Bad People and Bad Groups target old people that they believe have money, property, or something else they want. They push everyone else out of their life to make sure that when that person dies, they inherit everything of value, so this isn't a danger that stops. Ever.

With kids, groups or individual people can do the same thing. They can make you believe your parents and friends don't care about you. Even the most loving parents and best friends sometimes do and say things that can sound like they don't care. That includes saying "I don't care!" because that almost certainly means they don't care about the subject, not you as a person, but a Bad Person can make it feel like it's about you. Then they can get you to give them your things—computer, car, college savings, bank savings, etc. Sometimes the group that does this is a gang that then gets you to go further and commit crimes. Don't let that happen.

Cults

Sometimes the person or group trying to isolate you is a kind of religion called a cult. Cults demand you worship their leader as God. If anyone demands you worship a living person as God, run as far and as fast as you can and never, ever go near them again either in real life or online. Cults are *dangerous*.

Cult's first choice of prey is socially isolated people. This may be the normal short-term isolation that can happen when we are angry and shut out others, but cults are skilled at manipulation. They can exploit this momentary weakness and turn it into months, years, or even a lifetime split from those who love and care about us, as discussed above.

Family Dangers and Abuse

It isn't a secret that parents are human, and some of them are bad people. It is incredibly rare that they do anything really bad, but it happens. I recently found out about a classmate who was abused horribly by her entire extended family starting in elementary school. The abuse goes back generations, with each new generation being taught this is "normal" by their parents and grandparents. No one knew so we couldn't help. Now, she is helping others.

Child Protective Services (CPS) was created to help children whose are in dangerous situations, like my classmate, but they are what is called a double-edged sword. That means that bad things can happen with the best of intentions. It is important to be very, very certain there is a real reason to be concerned before you turn someone in for child abuse or neglect. Part of that is talking to adults and not doing it yourself because adults may know something you don't. For example, they may know that your friend has bruises all over their body not because they are being abused, but because they are sick and the disease, the treatment, or the medicine makes them bruise easily. The truth is, there are many simple explanations that you may not see. However, had anyone known and called CPS to my classmate's home, she could have been saved from a horrible situation.

The hardest thing I have done in my entire life was calling the home of a high school classmate and telling her parents she was talking about taking a long trip and not coming back and I was afraid she might commit suicide. While that is a different issue, the difficulty of making that call is comparable to telling an adult you are worried that someone is being abused. will never leave me. Thankfully, it was before caller ID so I was able to make the call anonymously. I have no idea what her parents did after that call, but I do know she was in a different school the next semester.

If you are in a situation where you have concerns about your own safety or that of a friend or classmate, <u>please talk to your parents, school counselor, church pastor, or youth pastor for help</u>. That is not a situation you can, or should, attempt to handle without help.

Online

Most people are not dangerous and are as afraid of you being a criminal as you are of them being a criminal. The ones who are criminals tend to follow certain patterns. Not all of them do these things, but there are definitely some big red flags (warning of danger) if someone does them. These are discussed in more detail in Chapter 13.

Finding Help

Saying "find help" is really easy, but actually talking to an adult and asking them for help is *not* easy–and it isn't easy for most adults either. Practice makes it less difficult, but asking for help when you really need it–even from someone you trust–can feel like a sign of weakness, even though it isn't. When you ask for help, you are admitting there is something you can't do. The truth is that no one can do everything, we all need help with some things. It is incredibly arrogant to think otherwise, and most people are flattered by the trust you are showing them when you ask for help.

Hopefully you trust your parents enough to go to them first when you need adult help, but if you don't, or if they don't listen, then find someone else. Other relatives (grandparents, aunts, uncles, older siblings, etc.), trusted family friends, coaches, Scout leader, youth group leaders, teachers, and school counselors are all possibilities. If that person doesn't help, it's OK to find another person and ask them, and keep going until someone does help.

Before you ask for help, take a few minutes to think through what you need help with and why it's a problem, then take a few minutes to mentally rehearse how you want the conversation to go. It can be as simple as, "Ashley took my yoyo and the teacher confiscated it." Then, before you get scared and back out of it, start the conversation. The only step you really need to take by yourself is telling the adult there is a problem. They should help you through the rest of it.

Think about it: when you start crying, looking upset, or being angry, your parents will often demand to know why whether you want to tell them or not. Once they know there is a real problem, they will talk to you and ask questions until they get the whole story. And they will do their best to make you feel better.

Activity

Introduce yourself to someone new, remembering to give a good strong (but not too strong!) handshake.

Quick Quiz

T/F   Worshipping a living human being as God is a good idea.

T/F   Some groups try to make people believe their family and friends don't care about them, even though they do.

T/F   Ask for help when you think there is Stranger Danger.

T/F   Red flags are things that warn of probable impending danger.

T/F   Cults and gangs are two kinds of Stranger Danger.

Resources

Articles

A History of Online Dating
www.eharmony.com/history-of-online-dating/

Online Safety for Teens: Are Internet Friends a Good Thing?
www.ibtimes.com/online-safety-teens-are-internet-friends-good-thing-2052238

The Seven Signs You're In a Cult
www.theatlantic.com/national/archive/2014/06/the-seven-signs-youre-in-a-cult/361400/

Virtual People, Real Friends
www.theguardian.com/commentisfree/2009/jan/02/internet-relationships

What Really Constitutes an Online Friend
www.liveabout.com/what-really-constitutes-an-online-friend-1385663

Videos

"Alyssa Lies"
www.youtube.com/watch?v=nLh5vbBLpxI

MEETING MY ONLINE BEST FRIEND!
www.youtube.com/watch?v=8FreBoPWKLc

{Part 4}
Traveling

Virtually all people travel to some degree, even if it's only to the grocery store and back home. Because we are safe so much of the time when we are traveling, most of us tend to take for granted that we will stay safe on all our trips and don't even take the most rudimentary safety steps, such as carrying a car emergency bag and reading the safety information on the back of hotel room doors. This section is all about keeping yourself safe when you are away from home.

Location Awareness: If you don't know where you are, how can you get to where you are going? You can't. It's really as simple as that. Without any location awareness, you will wander aimlessly, lost, until you happen to stumble upon either your destination or someone who can help you. Location awareness also means being aware of what is going on around you. For example, when you are driving, that includes other cars, bicyclists, pedestrians, and critters that may dart in front of your car or otherwise be a potential danger.

Driving: Most people learn when they are 16, if not slightly before, but even younger kids may need to drive in a true emergency. If you are wondering how someone younger than 16 can legally learn to drive, the answer is that a driver's license is usually specifically required on public roads, which means you can legally drive on some private property, such as your own driveway. (There is an article in Resources that goes into more detail on this.) You can also learn things like changing gears, turning on the wipers, and other basic tasks without ever moving the car.

Basic Auto Maintenance: Can you change a tire? The oil? Can you change the filters? What routine maintenance does your vehicle need?

On the Road: At home, you simply know a great many things that help you stay safe. You know where the windows and doors are, and you know which ones you can exit out of in an emergency. If one bedroom has a porch roof under it to make escape easier and another doesn't, you know that. On a trip, take a few minutes to look around and learn the safest ways to escape in an emergency.

If You Are Lost: It happens, even to adults. Do you know what to do and who to ask for help if you are lost? How is it different if you are at a big event like a carnival versus at the mall or on a road in the car? How does having (or not having) a cell signal change what you can do?

{FIFTEEN}

LOCATION AWARENESS

Put down the electronics and observe where you are wherever you may travel. Again, to be clear, *turn off the electronics and watch the road and your surroundings, even if you aren't the driver.* This is a theme throughout this entire series, not just this section on traveling: be aware of what is going on around you. It's critical for staying safe, and it's the foundation of location awareness.

The simplest way to think of it may be like this: imagine you are in a zombie movie or something like that. What things would keep you safe, and what make put you in danger? In real life, there's no need to panic or get too wrapped up about this, but it is a good idea to at least pay some attention to what's around you. The more dangerous the area seems, the more attention you need to pay.

In a Building

Did you ever notice that most movie theaters have a door near the movie screen, off to one or both sides? Those are emergency exit doors, and most buildings have them somewhere. (It's the law.) In an emergency, *you should use them.* That is what they are for. Many have automatic alarms attached to them, so don't use them unless it is an emergency. Sometimes, building owners are afraid people will sneak in through those exit doors, or sneak out without paying their bill, so they lock or chain them shut so no one inside can open them. This is *extremely* illegal and dangerous. If you see that, tell someone in charge. If they do not fix it immediately, report the incident to your local police dispatch so they can follow up to be sure it is fixed. The article "10 Modern Night Club Fires" (in Resources) shows exactly why it is so very dangerous and should be reported and fixed immediately.

Be aware of the nearest exit, and the next-nearest, and anything that might block your way. Think about which areas are safe or not, and what impact potential disasters could have on that. If there is a large glass-filled area, that could become very dangerous in an earthquake or other natural disaster. What other things are near you that could be dangerous, or could help you stay safe? Are there any animals (such as pets) that could be a danger?

In a Vehicle

It is impossible to be aware of your location if you entire focus is on a tablet, phone, or other electronic device. Even if it's not electronic, if your focus is on knitting, reading, talking, or napping, you will not be aware of your location. Look out the window and notice what's there.

- Street and route signs.
- Odd intersections and turns.
- Giant or unusual plants or trees.
- Billboards.
- Building names.
- Unusual stores or buildings. A gas station is not unusual. A two-story gas station with a two-story gas pump outside it would be unusual.
- Artwork, including statues and murals on buildings.
- Roadwork, including detours and closed roads that might impact your return trip.
- Areas where the traffic is moving slowly or "stacking up", which might be good to avoid on your return trip.

- Major highways or big streets.

It is also important to notice what is on and around the road. Deer are notorious for running in front of cars. The deer die, the cars are badly damaged, and the people in the car can be injured. And where there is one deer, there is usually a family. If you see a deer run out and you are driving, slow down and make sure there aren't more waiting to run across the road. Some roads have a lot of bicyclists or runners. The list of potential distractions and dangers from the side of the road is enormous, so just pay attention.

Large Groups

Notice how any larger groups of people you encounter behave.

- If they are all moving in one direction, odds are good that roads in that direction will soon be blocked for a while.
- If fists are being raised in the air and people are starting to shout, it might be dangerous in mere minutes. Leave quickly and don't come back that day.
- If the group is getting larger and larger (more people joining and walking toward it), then avoid the area when you leave. Even if it isn't dangerous, it will be very crowded.
- If the crowd is dispersing (people leaving in all directions), it will probably be OK to come back through shortly but the roads all around will have distracted pedestrians while they are dispersing, and a larger than usual number of cars for a while after that.

Use your eyes and ears to gather information to help stay safe.

Walking

If you are walking or in a complex of buildings such as a large shopping center or a school campus, pay attention to where you are and how to get back to where you started.

- Do you pass any odd looking buildings or statues?
- Is there any artwork, including graffiti, that stands out?
- Where are ponds, streams, or other water features?
- Are there any areas that make you feel unsafe, including alleys or places with a large group of people? Can you avoid them both ways or at least coming back?
- Where are there "trap points" (Chapter 21)?
- Are there posted maps to help you find your way? Where? Do you know where you are and where you are going on those maps?

If there are paper or electronic maps to help find your way, it's a good idea to pick one up or download it. In addition to finding your way there and back, you may find other spots listed that you want to visit. The same goes for maps of any buildings you visit. In particular, museums tend to have them. (That's how I found the Ice Cream Parlor in the Museum of American History, before the café closed.)

Once you arrive at a location, pay attention to where you are within the building, or buildings. If you need to go to the bathroom or have a drink of water, can you find what you need quickly? If you get separated from your friends and family, where can you find them again? If the lights go out, how will you find your way out? Most buildings have emergency lighting, but the faster you can move, the less likely you are to be trapped in a group of panicked people.

Activity

For one day, do not use electronics, read, or do anything else that prevents you from looking out the window while you are traveling, including on the bus. Observe everywhere you go. Write down new things you notice out the window. At the end of the day, see how much you learned about your area just by looking out the window.

Quick Quiz

T/F   Locked, chained emergency exits are no cause for alarm.

T/F   Billboards, artwork, and other unusual items are helpful for location awareness.

T/F   Even common buildings like gas stations can be good markers if there is something very unusual about them.

T/F   Location awareness doesn't matter if someone is driving you.

T/F   It is a good idea to really watch where you are going so you can find your way back.

Resources

Articles

10 Modern Night Club Fires
listverse.com/2010/03/08/top-10-modern-night-club-fires

Being Aware of Your Surroundings Can Drastically Reduce Safety Incidents
blog.psionline.com/talent/aware-of-surroundings-can-reduce-safety-incidents

Essential Safety for Kids: Staying Safe on the Streets
www.netmums.com/lifestyle/house-and-home/essential-safety-for-kids/essential-safety-for-kids-staying-safe-on-the-stre

How to Be More Mentally Aware
www.wikihow.com/Be-More-Mentally-Aware

Exit Routes
www.osha.gov/OshDoc/data_General_Facts/emergency-exit-routes-factsheet.pdf

Books

Can I See Your Hands: A Guide to Situational Awareness, Personal Risk Management, Resilience and Security by Gavriel Schneider

Sheep No More: The Art of Awareness and Attack Survival by Jonathan T. Gilliam

Situational Awareness 101:Because What You Don't Know Can Hurt You! by Jay Johnson

Situational Sense: Basic Threat Detection Using Situational Awareness and Common Sense by Matthew Dermody

Scouting-Specific

Safety Merit Badge
meritbadge.org/wiki/index.php/Safety

Videos

Tim Kennedy Teaches Fundamentals of Situational Awareness! | Sheepdog Response
www.youtube.com/watch?v=oPG1SPwvot4

{SIXTEEN}

DRIVING

No one is encouraging you to break the law, but what would happen if a fourteen year old went hiking or hunting and the only adult with them had a heart attack or broke a leg? There might not be a cell signal and simply waiting for help to arrive could be a disaster. If the younger teen basically knew how to drive a car, even if they did it at slow speed, they could get the adult to help or at least reach a cell signal. The Resources section of this chapter includes an article about a ten year old boy who took control of the truck he was in when the driver had a diabetic attack, thereby saving multiple lives. Police hailed him as a hero. So while it's not likely to happen, it might.

Personally, I think my tween *could* drive because he has played a driving game with a console that uses brakes and gas on the floor as well as a steering wheel, and their Dad and I talk to our kids a lot about driving skills and good driving habits a lot. For example, we have talked about how important it is to slow down going around corners because you can't see what is coming toward you or if there is a dangerous obstruction like a tree branch or dead deer on the road. I am equally certain that I would need to be in imminent danger of death to hand over my keys to him!

Once you get the hang of it, driving isn't too hard, but it does take practice. Clearly, anyone who doesn't have their license will be an inexperienced, just plain bad, driver, particularly when freaked out by an injured adult, but this chapter is assuming someone is in a potential life-or-death situation and there is no other choice to help keep them alive, or that you are already old enough to drive legally.

Brakes

Vehicles have two kinds of brakes. One is a parking brake. It isn't always used, but the car either can't be driven at all or may be damaged if it is driven with the parking brake on. A light that says "BRAKE" usually lights up on the console when it is on. The most common locations for it are in the center console, on the drivers' floor near the outside of the car, and on the console near the driver's left knee. Learn where the parking brake is on your family vehicles and how to set *and release* each one.

The second kind is used every time a car is driven. It is a wide pedal near the driver's feet used to slow down and stop the vehicle.

Gas

This is the long, narrow pedal on the right side near the driver's feet. It makes the car go faster. Don't push the gas and brakes at the same time. It's bad for the car.

Flashers/Hazard Lights

Know how to turn them on and off, and keep them on while you are driving if you are an underage driver driving in an emergency because if you are not a licensed driver, you are automatically a hazard. Licensed drivers should *not* drive with this on unless there is damage to their vehicle or they are otherwise signaling a danger. There is normally a red button with a triangle on it to symbolize the "flashers" for the car somewhere easy to see and reach on the dashboard. Most commonly, it is in the center of the front console, under the radio, so either the driver or front passenger can reach it.

The flashers are essentially both turn signals flashing at the same time. It's a way to let other vehicles know there is something wrong. It could be that the car is driving slowly due to mechanical difficulty, but it generally indicates a car that is going slowly. It could also indicate a car that is accelerating out of control or no longer has functional brakes. If there is a sudden slow-down or obstruction, you can turn on the flashers for a minute so cars behind you notice and slow down without hitting you. When other cars see the flashers, they will know to be extra cautious around your vehicle. In an emergency where the driver is inexperienced and freaked out and the passenger is in critical condition, this is a very good thing.

Mirrors

The driver always needs to adjust the mirrors when they get into the car. The mirrors are what let you see behind and around the car, including vehicles approaching in other traffic lanes. Adjusting mirrors while driving isn't a great choice for an experienced driver. For one with no real road experience, it could be a fatal mistake. Be sure to adjust them before starting. If you need to adjust them again, stop at a stop sign or traffic light, or pull off to the side of the road first.

Stick Shift

If anyone in your family regularly drives a stick, they need to explain to you how it works and at what points to change the gears. You should write the information down and keep it in the car because in an emergency, you probably won't remember when to shift without having that reminder. To be clear: read and review it *before* you start to drive, not while driving, just like with mirrors.

Reaching Help

As soon as you find help, stop the car and put it in P(ark). This may be another car, an occupied home, or an open store. It might even be a person you see running or walking a dog. Immediately explain what happened, why you were driving, and ask for help. Follow their instructions. They may need you to continue driving and follow them, or they may need to have you change seats so they can drive. If they have a car full of their own children, they can't exactly leave them abandoned, which is just one example of why someone can't simply leave their car or home unattended.

Activity

Sit in the car while it is turned off. Push on the gas and brake pedals to see how they feel. Turn the key in the ignition to learn how to start it. Without moving the vehicle, change gears from P(ark) to R(everse) to D(rive). Try to turn off the car and remove the key while it's in D. (It won't work.) Then put it back to R and P. Now remove the key.

Quick Quiz

T/F   Once you know the basics of driving, it's OK to jump in a car and drive any time you want.

T/F   As soon as you have your license, you can drive just as well as adults with decades of driving experience.

T/F   Telling your grandparents you learned how to drive underage is a good thing.

T/F   NEVER turn on the flashers while you (an inexperienced, underage driver) are driving in an emergency.

T/F   Turn off the car and remove the key while it's in D(rive).

Resources

Articles

10 Year Old Boy Prevents Accident by Taking Control of a Truck
www.dailymail.co.uk/news/article-3511985/Alabama-s-Christopher-Wheeler-10-hailed-hero-weaving-CONTROL-speeding-truck-Interstate-traffic-terrifying-10-mile-drama.html

Car Talk: Learn to Drive Stick
www.cartalk.com/content/learn-drive-stick-3

Easiest Way to Learn How to Drive a Manual Transmission or Stick Shift Car
axleaddict.com/safety/Easiest-Way-to-Learn-How-to-Drive-Manual

How to Drive
www.wikihow.com/Drive

How to Drive a Stick Shift
www.dmv.org/how-to-guides/driving-stick.php

Laws Regarding Driving on Private Property
legalbeagle.com/6499776-laws-regarding-driving-private-property.html

Books

How Cars Work by Tom Newton

How to Drive a Car: Parallel Parking and Driving Maneuvers Made Easy by Hank Wysocki

Learn How to Drive and Survive by Linda Ann Azarela

Learn to Drive (the Complete Version) by Joseph Collins ADI

The Driving Book: Everything New Drivers Need to Know but Don't Know How to Ask by Karen Gravelle

Other

School Driving 3D (app)

Scouting-Specific

*Traffic Safety Merit Badge
meritbadge.org/wiki/index.php/Traffic_Safety

{Seventeen}

Basic Auto Maintenance

There are some simple auto maintenance chores everyone should be able to do. Checking tire pressure, changing a tire, checking the oil and fluids, conditions of belts and hoses, and changing filters are a few of those. You should also learn how to wash a car properly and really look at the car's condition while you do it.

First Steps

These steps will help keep you safe no matter what maintenance you are doing, and the first step is immobilizing your vehicle. You *really* don't want your vehicle moving while you are underneath it. Be sure your vehicle is safely, and completely, out of traffic. That doesn't just mean not on a road. Street parking is not generally a safe choice, even though the car is safely out of traffic, because there are simply too many other vehicles moving too close to it. If you are forced to do any work on the side of the road, including changing a tire or adding oil, turn on your hazard lights.

If your car doesn't have enough clearance for you to comfortably work underneath, then you need to either drive it up onto ramps or use jacks to lift the car up. Put wheel/chock blocks behind the wheels, if possible, to further ensure they don't move. In an emergency, you can use large rocks, pieces of wood, or anything else you can find that is large and strong enough. Once there is enough clearance and the car is level, put it in park, turn it off, remove the keys, and apply the parking brake. If you are near traffic, don't forget the hazard lights as well.

It is a very good idea to take the time to learn the "jacking points" for your vehicle before you have an emergency. When you jack up the car, the jack stands will go on these jacking points. These are slightly stronger spots designed for this purpose. If you use a jack in the wrong place, you may dent or otherwise damage your vehicle. The first car I ever bought new ended up with a dent in the trunk from a jack that was positioned slightly wrong. A decade later, it still made me sad to see—and that was after it was totaled in an accident! Take the time to find the information, then photocopy the information and keep it in your car. Take a picture with your phone and favorite it so you have a copy there as well. If you ever need it, you will be glad it's so easy to find.

Don't touch the engine if it is still hot. If it has been running for more than a few minute/miles, give it a few minutes to cool off so you don't get burnt. When you pop open the hood, hold your bare (not gloved) hand out toward the engine. As you move it toward whatever part you need to touch, you should be able to feel if it is too hot before you touch it and get burnt. If it is still too hot, give it a few more minutes.

Change an Air Filter

There are three primary filters: air, oil, and fuel filters. Changing your oil filter is discussed in the next section. Changing the fuel filter is an easy DIY task with many older cars, but newer ones can require multiple expensive, single-use tools. It is probably not going to be one of the first tasks you do yourself, but it is a good one to keep in mind as you become more confident.

Changing the air filter, in particular, is incredibly easy on most cars, and a good first task to try to build confidence. Easy doesn't mean unimportant! You need to read the owner's manual for specifics on your vehicle and start with the "First Steps" above. These are the basic steps, although changing filters may not require the car to be lifted as described in First Steps. Check your owner's manual for filter specifications and make sure you have a new one ready to put in before you start.

To change your air filter, open the hood and find the air filter unit. Remove the air filter cover. Before you can remove the old filter, you will probably need to loosen the hose clamp on the air conduct and remove the screws or wing nuts that hold the air filter cover in place. **Put them carefully to the side so you don't lose them.** Now you can remove the air filter. (If you can't, replace everything and ask for help before you damage your car.) Clean the air filter housing, put the new filter in, and replace the cover. It's as simple as that.

Change the Oil and Oil Filter

If you only learn two auto maintenance skills, learn how to check the oil and fluids. Start with the "First Steps" listed above.

Gather the supplies you need: an oil drain pan, a box end or socket wrench to remove the drain plug, an oil filter wrench, a funnel, a jack, jack stands or ramps (depending on the vehicle's ground clearance), and latex or rubber gloves. You will also need oil, a new oil filter, and possibly a new drain plug. Your owner's manual will specify the type and amount of oil needed. When you are buying oil, remember that you have to lift and pour from the container. A single five-quart container might seem tempting but end up more difficult to handle than five single-quart containers. Double-check the type of oil before starting the oil change too. 5W-20 and 5W-30 are *not* the same.

If you don't already know where to find the oil drain plug for your car, take the time to find that in the owner's manual or online before starting. It should also let you know if there is an undercover that needs removed. This is a good time to find a place to recycle the oil when you are done because it cannot either go in regular household garbage or be poured out. Google "car oil disposal" to find locations where it can be cleaned and recycled.

Turn your car on and let it run for two or three minutes. (The colder the weather, the longer it takes.) The goal is to make the oil warm enough to flow out easily but not hot enough to burn you. Setting (parked) allows dirt and sediments to settle, and those are what you really need to remove. Running the engine mixes those sediments back into the oil just like shaking a bottle of salad dressing mixes everything back together, so when the oil flows out, it removes the dirt and sediments as well.

Place the oil drain pan underneath the car. Put on nitrile or other similar gloves. Open the hood and remove the oil cap. Find the oil pan and the drain plug located under the engine. The transmission drain plug is often attached to the exhaust; don't open it by accident. Position the drain pan under the drain plug. Remove the drain plug. Metal washers can be reused, but felt or paper drain plug gaskets should be removed and replaced. Try not to drop any of these items into the drain pan, which will soon be filled with oil.

Wait while the oil drains out. It will take several minutes. While this is happening, start inspecting and cleaning the drain, plug, and gasket. Put the new gasket on the drain plug and replace the plug. DO NOT move the drain pan yet.

Find the oil filter and slowly unscrew it without fully removing it. (This may necessitate using a tool.) Oil will probably spill out of the oil filter, which is why the drain pan still needs to be under the car. Wrap a plastic bag around the oil filter and set it upside down to drain while you finish the process.

Use your gloved finger to smear some of the replacement oil on the new filter's gasket ring to lubricate it, create a good seal, and make it easier to remove next time. You can pour some oil into the chamber before adding the filter to help it refill and start to circulate more quickly. Tighten the new filter, being careful not to cross-thread it. The filter box will give specific instructions.

Now it's time to add the new oil. Every drop of oil will not have drained out, especially since a jacked up car is rarely level, so add about one quart less than the recommended amount. The remaining quart will be added later. Put the oil cap back on and run the engine for about thirty seconds. Check under the engine for any leaks. If there are none, remove the oil pan and remove the car from the jack stands or ramps. When it is back on level ground, re-check the levels and finish filling the oil.

Put the used oil needs in a container that seals for transport and disposal. Milk jugs work well, but make sure it's clear that oil, not food, is in the container. Many auto parts stores recycle used oil at no cost. If you use a container (like a milk jug) that isn't designed to hold oil, it may start to break down and eventually leak, so try to get the oil somewhere for recycling fairly quickly.

Change a Tire

If you only learn one auto maintenance skill, learn how to change a tire. Start with the "First Steps" listed above.

Take the jack, a lug wrench, and your spare tire out of the trunk. (Take time to make sure you always have these in your car and that they are in good shape.) Put the hubcap in the car as soon as you remove it to reduce the chances of forgetting and losing it. Hubcaps aren't cheap.

Use the wrench to loosen all the lug nuts but don't remove them yet. Use the jack to lift the car off the ground. The owner's manual may tell you the best points to position the jack for your specific vehicle. (If you put it in a spot that isn't strong enough, you can damage the body.) The tires should be about six inches off the ground when you finish. Now remove the lug nuts and pull the tire straight out to remove it. Place the lug nuts in a pile to be sure you won't lose one. Lay the tire on the ground under the car, just in case the jack fails.

Place the spare all the way on the car, being sure it is tightly fitted. Put the lug nuts back on and lower the car to the ground. Double check that the lug nuts are tight. Replace all the items in the trunk, including the damaged tire, which might be reparable, and the hubcap, if it isn't already there. Repairing a tire that is otherwise in good condition is generally cheaper than replacing it. (Using Fix-a-Flat is a good fix in a true emergency, but it tends to make it impossible to repair a tire, meaning it must be replaced.)

If you are using an emergency spare tire like the ones that often come with cars, it is important to remove it fairly quickly but to drive fairly slowly while it is on. Most are designed to be driven under 100 miles at under 50 mph because they are only intended for short-term emergency use. This means that even if the speed limit where you are driving is 70 mph, you need to drive 50 mph, just keep your hazard lights on to warn other drivers of your slow speed.

Check the Tire Pressure

The ideal tire pressure changes when it's either hot or cold outside so it is important to check pressure every few months. The owner's manual and inside of the driver's side car door should both list the ideal pressure when the tires are cold. This pressure, or PSI, is the lowest the tire pressure should ever be. The manual will also list the ideal PSI in hot weather, and if the front and back tires should have the same or different pressures. (You can use the same basic process to inflate bike tires.) Having tires that are either over or under-inflated can be dangerous, so even though this is a quick and easy, it is important.

Once you know the ideal pressure, either get your air pump out or go to a gas station with an air pump. Either way, use your own air pressure gauge to get the most accurate readings rather than a potentially unreliable or broken one. It is easiest and most efficient if you check the pressure on all four tires before adjusting the pressure on any of them. Keep in mind that driving and sitting in sunlight both cause tires to heat up. Tires are generally cold enough to check when it has been at least three hours since being driven, and they start warming up in as little as one mile of driving. If you can't reach a gas station with an air pump in less than one mile, then you should check the tire pressure before you start driving.

Unscrew the valve stem cap and remove it from the valve on the first tire. Put the air pressure gauge on to check the current pressure. If there is a hissing sound, the gauge is too loose. Tighten it before proceeding, maintaining even pressure as you push the gauge on. If the pressure is too low, you will need to add air. If it is too high, you will need to release some air. Once this is done, replace the valve stem cap and proceed to check the remaining tires.

Don't forget to check the air pressure in your spare tire as well.

Wash a Car

This seems pretty self-evident, and the basics are, but if you want to keep the paint really nice, then take the time to learn a bit more. The basic steps are rinse, wash, rinse, dry, wax. "Rinse" means "to wash lightly." Do not use high-powered spray; it can damage the paint. During this process, try to park in the shade so the sun doesn't dry your car before you can. That may leave water marks and soap stains.

The first rinse should remove debris like leaves, dust, and possibly some (but not all) the mud and road salt. Washing will remove most of the rest. Start at the top and work your way down.

When you are washing it, start with the wheels, being sure to use a specialized product and a brush designed for cleaning wheels and spokes. Use several buckets (ideally three – one each for clean soapy water, rinse water, and wheels) to keep from putting the dirt right back on the car and to keep the harsher products used for your wheels and hubcaps away from the paint.

Wash the car using car washing detergent, not dish washing detergent from the kitchen that can strip off protective, built up layers of wax and damage rubber seals. Most car washing detergents only require a capful mixed into a bucket of water. Microfiber towels or sheepskin work well for washing it. Dry it with a waffle-weave drying towel or chamois cloth. Be careful with chamois since it can scratch the paint. House towels of all sorts can leave tiny scratches in the paint, so try not to use them. Once you are done washing, rinse the car again. Repeat if necessary.

Finally, dry the car and wax it, if needed. If water beads on the wet car, the wax is fine and you can stop cleaning the exterior. If not, it's time to wax. The protective coat of wax keeps the paint underneath looking better.

Detailing

Detailing cars goes a step (or five) beyond just washing them. Exterior detailing can make your vehicle look like new again. Interior detailing is a much deeper, more thorough clean than just wiping everything down and giving it a quick vacuum. As an example of the extra steps taken in detailing, a clay bar can be used to help clean the vehicle. This specialized clay bar (definitely not modeling or craft clay) grabs ahold of any dirt, grit, or other residue a simple wash leaves behind and removes it without damaging the paint.

Dealerships normally detail used cars before trying to sell them to get the best possible price. People detail their cars to keep them in the best possible condition and, of course, looking good.

Activity

Choose a task from this chapter and try it.

Quick Quiz

T/F   You should use dishwashing detergent to wash cars.

T/F   Checking your owner's manual is one of the first steps for many kinds of routine maintenance.

T/F   Changing an air filter is much more complex than changing a fuel filter on most cars.

T/F   The first step is parking your vehicle in a safe location.

T/F   A car's spare tire can be run as many miles and at the same speeds as a regular tire.

Resources

Articles

Guide to Detailing
www.guidetodetailing.com/detailing-101/

How to Change a Tire
www.bridgestonetire.com/tread-and-trend/drivers-ed/how-to-change-a-flat-tire

How to Change Your Air Filter
www.allstate.com/tools-and-resources/car-insurance/change-car-air-filter.aspx

How to Change Your Oil
www.edmunds.com/how-to/how-to-change-your-oil-the-real-down-and-dirty.html

How to Check Air Pressure
www.wikihow.com/Check-Air-Pressure-in-Tires

How Long Can You Really Use Your Spare Tire
www.popularmechanics.com/cars/how-to/a3254/how-long-can-you-really-use-your-spare-tire-7710515/

How to Properly Wash and Dry a Car
www.detailedimage.com/Ask-a-Pro/how-to-properly-wash-and-dry-a-car/

Books

Auto Upkeep: Basic Car Care, Maintenance, and Repair by Michael F. Gray and Linda E. Gray

Automotive Detailing Manual (Haynes Techbook) by Haynes

D.I.Y. – Detail it Yourself: The Car Enthusiast's Guide to a Fantastic Looking Car by Joey Monroe

Girls Auto Clinic Glove Box Guide by Patrice Banks

Women's Car DIY: The Multi-Tasker's Manual by Caroline Lake

Other

Air Pressure Gauge

Detailing Kit

Wheel Chocks

Scouting-Specific

Automotive Maintenance Merit Badge
meritbadge.org/wiki/index.php/Automotive_Maintenance

Car Care Badge
forgirls.girlscouts.org/home/badgeexplorer/#car-care

Videos

How to Change a Tire – change a flat car tire step by step
www.youtube.com/watch?v=joBmbh0AGSQ

How to Change Your Air Filter
www.youtube.com/watch?v=OuAH8lpgDrk

How to: Check Tire Pressure and Inflate Tires
www.youtube.com/watch?v=QTst6ZdlVtg

{Eighteen}

On the Road

"Bugging out" means leaving in a hurry, especially in an emergency situation. In common usage, it tends to mean there is a SHTF (Stuff Hits the Fan) situation severe enough to make it unsafe or impossible to stay put. To stay safe, people need to take all the supplies they can manage and leave for a (usually predetermined) safe location. With bugging out, it is entirely possible you will never return home. There might not be a home to return to, or it might not be something you could live in. Mold and water damage often leaves homes uninhabitable even if they are still standing.

"Evacuation" is the next most severe possibility. When a serious weather event, forest fire, or other danger is an imminent threat, the government may issue an evacuation order. These should never be ignored. You may believe that you will be safe, and you may even be right, but you might be wrong and the consequences of being wrong are potentially deadly. More importantly, vital resources are wasted in every evacuation either trying to convince hesitant people to leave or rescuing them after disaster strikes. Staying put can place others in harm's way, even if you are ultimately safe staying put. As with bugging out, you may not have a home to return to.

Getting home safely should be your first priority if a disaster occurs in an area you are visiting/on vacation. Hurricane, tornado, and earthquake prone areas in particular often have published evacuation plans. These are a good place to start. Depending on the problem and your location, it is possible that garage doors (parking lots) will automatically lock, with cars stuck in them, within fifteen minutes or so of a disaster being declared. If your car is inside, runs out of gas, or is otherwise unusable, you will need to be prepared to find alternate transportation.

Basic Map Reading

Maps and finding your way are covered in more detail in *26 Outdoor Life Skills* in this series, but the basics are simple enough to be taught in a Dr. Seuss book. A Compass Rose shows the four cardinal section—north, south, east, and west. Maps have a scale to show how far apart things are. The scale changes from map to map, so you must always check the scale included on the map you are using. Different symbols and colors show different things, like blue for water and a tent for campsites. Every map has a key to explain the symbols used on that map.

If you are traveling and not using a GPS, including your phone, you are probably using a street or road map, including ones printed from online maps. These show all the roads in an area and may include other information such as one-way streets, special buildings (churches, libraries, schools), and transportation hubs (train stations, bus stations, airports). If you have any warning about an impending disaster, you should try to print out maps for the areas you will travel through to get home/out of the area. In an emergency, you can't count on a cell signal or GPS to guide you. Consider it a bonus if you do have a signal. That means you can't count on any map app on your phone to guide you and you will need to rely on what you know and physical, paper maps.

In a Car

Always consider traffic in your planning, even in areas where traffic isn't usually an issue. In an evacuation, it is important to allow for the realities of traffic. Leaving early and quickly should help avoid the worst traffic. If you are outside a big city, the giant traffic clog will probably take longer to reach you, but it inevitably will. Try to be on the road before it does.

Once you are ready to leave, be sure to wear your safety belt, properly, and sit, properly, in your seat. If your safety belt does not go across your waist AND from your shoulder across your chest to your waist on the other side of your body without hanging loosely or pulling so tightly that you cannot move, then you are not wearing it properly. If your behind is not on the seat cushion with your back upright and against the seat back, then you are not sitting properly in your seat. If you aren't sitting properly, the car safety features can't work properly, and emergency services vehicles like ambulances can't get through traffic clogs easily and are already stretched thin in emergencies. Even if the emergency hasn't hit yet (like an incoming hurricane), emergency services are preparing and getting rest before the massive post-disaster workload hits.

Do not touch the driver. That means no poking, playing with hair, kicking the seat back, or otherwise jostling their body and disturbing them. No yelling in the car. No throwing anything in the car. It doesn't matter how long, boring, or slow the drive. These can all distract the driver and potentially lead to an accident.

In a Car Accident

Pull over to the side of the road. If you are on a major highway, you may need to pull into the median in the center, but getting out of traffic quickly is important. It is also important to be near any other vehicles involved in the accident because you have to exchange insurance information. These means that you each give the other person your name and phone number, your insurance company's name and phone number, and your insurance policy number. The insurance company of the person who is determined to be "at fault" will have to pay bills for both parties. What they pay (vehicle repairs, rental car during repairs, medical bills) is determined by what coverage that person has.

If you are in an accident, don't just jump out of your vehicle. Move a little slowly to be sure you aren't injured. It isn't unusual for adrenalin to mask pain at first, even for major injuries. If it does, moving too much and too fast can make things worse. At the same time, if you are told to either stay put or get out fast, do so, especially if it's by emergency services.

If it isn't a minor accident (fender-bender), call 911 to have the police and EMTs come to the scene. Call your parents/family to let them know what has happened and so they can pick you up or arrange for someone else to pick you up. Then call your insurance company to let them know what happened. You should always have your insurance card in your wallet and that has all the information you need, including the number to call in case of an accident and your policy number. They will probably give you the number for, or possibly call, a tow truck company to tow your vehicle to a garage they have a contract with. That garage will give an estimate to repair it.

The insurance company may "total" your vehicle . That means they declare it "totally" wrecked and won't pay to fix it. Instead, they will give you a check for the amount they think it is worth. You can argue with them a little about the value they declare it worth or to get it fixed instead of totaled, but know that their final decision is final and you will end up having to take what they give you. Once you receive a check for the amount to repair or replace your vehicle, it's your choice what to do with it. Sometimes, in a minor accident, you may choose not to do any repairs. If your car is totaled, you can choose to get a replacement that is similar to the old vehicle, or perhaps to upgrade to something newer and nicer.

In a Hotel

Most of us stay in hotels on vacation. (If you go camping, read my book *26 Outdoor Life Skills* in this series for ways to be prepared when camping.) Hotels can be over a hundred floors tall in very big cities, but most top out at four to six floors, which is easily walkable for almost anyone–certainly going down–and reachable for a fire truck ladder.

Hotels are just large buildings. Like any building, bad things can happen, including bad luck. Power outages, floods, fire, blizzards, tornadoes, civil unrest, and all manners of other problems can affect your stay, and you need a plan if that happens. The first step is knowing where you are. Every hotel room has a map on the back of the entry door or on the wall near it. That map shows your room location and directions to the closest emergency exit as well as the location of the elevator(s), other rooms, vending and ice machines, and anything else on the floor. That emergency route is the reason it is there. The law requires it so people know how to escape, and you should look at it. There may be other stairwells and routes out of the building that aren't marked on the map in your room, especially in large hotels that may only show a small portion of the floor on your map. Try asking the front desk to show or tell you where they are located. If they don't know or can't tell you for some reason, find them. Either way, take a few minutes to see where they are.

Take a moment to see if the stairwells have large banks of glass or skylights, if the doors are tricky at all, and anything else that might make it either harder or easier to use a particular staircase. Windows and skylights may shatter in an earthquake or tornado but also let in natural light (including moonlight), making it easier to move safely when the lights are out but also potentially dangerous in bare feet.

Most of us remember where the elevators are and more or less what they look like because we use them. Using the stairs a few times will help you remember where they are in an emergency, but even mentally repeating whether it is toward the elevators or away from them a few times helps.

It's a good idea to have a flashlight nearby in a hotel. The flashlight app on most phones is good enough to help you navigate through the room, down the hall, and down the stairway safely. It's also a good idea to bring a few easy-to-make snacks or meals. My family was once stuck in a hotel at the center of a fairly large power outage, right at dinner time. No restaurants or grocery stores were open because of the power outage (credit card scanners and registers weren't working) and we needed to eat. Luckily, I had oatmeal, cereal, and a few other items that were easy to make with just hot water, and there was hot water on hand for guests to make tea. Problem solved!

On a Plane

The first step is almost the same as in a hotel: Pay attention to the emergency information in the seat back in front of you. Know where the closest exits are and how to reach them. Listen to the emergency information the crew provides at the start of each flight, even if you are certain you already know it all. Keep the area around you clear of things that could fly up and hurt you if the plane hits a pocket of turbulence. (Just about anything can hurt you if the turbulence gets rough enough, so just keep everything put away.) Wear sensible shoes. Either keep them on the whole time or be able to put them on again very, very quickly.

Count the number of rows to the exit and move quickly if you are forced to abandon the plane. If you are in a plane crash, abandon all your stuff. Even taking a few seconds to grab non-essential items (including your phone, which isn't an essential item) or keep track of them during evacuation could be fatal.

On Public Transportation

Big cities normally have decent, sometimes even great, public transit. So does most of Europe. Trains, buses, and variations on the two such as light rail and subways are the main forms of public transportation. These have many scheduled stops along a route that is the same every day. If your destination isn't near a stop, then you exit at the closest stop and figure out a way to get there, possibly using a taxi or shuttle.

If you are using mass transit, definitely make sure you have a printed map. These are usually available online and can be downloaded, or simply look at the vehicle's walls to see if one is posted there. An electronic one is good, but a printed map isn't dependent on battery life. Either way, having a map is important to make it easier to get off at the right spot and make any necessary transfers.

If you need a transfer on a bus, tell the driver when you get on and they will give you a transfer slip. The fee will be added to the fare. For a subway, you normally simply get off, walk to the next train platform, and hop on that train. Most of the time the fare is automatically calculated based on the stations you use when you enter and leave the system. If you spend the entire day wandering around (lost) and end up exiting one station from where you entered, you pay as if you only went one stop.

Stand near the door when you are within one or possibly two stops of where you will leave, especially when it's crowded. If you don't, you risk being stuck and not getting to the door in time to exit. Then you need to find another way to get back on track. You also risk ending up in a neighborhood you do not want to be in. This doesn't necessarily mean a dangerous neighborhood. In a low-density neighborhood it may be hard to find a bus, taxi, etc. quickly.

There are also taxis and shuttle services, but those are a little different. Taxis and shuttles take one person or a few people directly from one point to another with no extra stops in the middle. There may be other scheduled stops, especially for shuttles that stop to pick up or drop off several people.

Activity

Pick someplace you visit regularly such as a relatives' home and plan a route and an alternate route from there back to your home. Try to have one route that relies on larger roads such as interstate highways and one that relies on secondary or back roads. If possible, have a third route that uses public transportation for most or all of the distance.

Quick Quiz

T/F   The map on the back of the hotel door, or on a wall near it, provides invaluable information in the event of a fire or other emergency.

T/F   If you have an electronic map, there is no conceivable reason you would need a paper one as well.

T/F   When you plan a trip, especially an evacuation, include time for traffic.

T/F   A compass rose shows latitude and longitude.

T/F   It is a good idea to listen to the safety briefing at the beginning of a flight even if you have flown before. Different aircraft may have slightly different information.

Resources

Articles

Different Types of Maps
mapgeeks.org/different-types-of-maps/

How to Read a Topo Map
www.rei.com/learn/expert-advice/topo-maps-how-to-use.html

How to Stay Safe in a Hotel
www.businessinsider.com/how-to-stay-safe-in-a-hotel-2016-3/?op=1

Map Reading for Beginners
www.thoughtco.com/map-reading-geography-1435601

Map Symbols
www.compassdude.com/map-symbols.php

What is Orienteering?
orienteeringusa.org/explore/

Books

Basic Illustrated Map and Compass by Cliff Jacobson and Lon Levin

Be Expert with Map and Compass, 3rd Ed. By Bjorn Kjellstrom and Carina Kjellstrom Elgin

Essential Wilderness Navigation by Craig Caudill and Tracy Trimble

Map Reading and Land Navigation:FM3-25.26 by the Department of the Army

There's a Map on My Lap by Dr. Seuss

Wilderness Navigation by Bob Burns

Other

Lensatic/Sighting Compass

Maps, Map Skills, Atlases: Free Games & Activities for kids
www.wartgames.com/themes/geography/maps.html

Orienteering Compass

Topographic and Street Maps for anywhere you travel often

Scouting-Specific

Traveler Badge
forgirls.girlscouts.org/home/badgeexplorer/#traveler

Videos

Hotel Safety Tips for Vacationers Travelers
www.youtube.com/watch?v=TLT69mK29DY

How to choose a Compass
www.youtube.com/watch?v=YErtztBYO38

How to make a compass when you get lost?
www.youtube.com/watch?v=fDrXNwuOONY

Make the Safe Choice – Be Aware of Your Surroundings
www.youtube.com/watch?v=Nfe6L22Uhdc

Orienteering. The basic way to use a map & compass
https://www.youtube.com/watch?v=qIelaDAerM8

{Nineteen}

If You Are Lost

With GPS systems ever-present in our cars, phones, and tablets, getting lost is less of a concern than it was in the past, but it still happens. Cell signals and GPS signals can be lost all too easily, especially in an emergency when circuits become overloaded or in isolated areas where there is no coverage (or none by your carrier) to begin with. We have all heard stories of people who became lost in a blizzard or when their car broke down in a remote area and they decided to walk to safety. Even with GPS, it is possible to get lost, it's just harder. Maps need to be kept updated, but even with the latest download installed mere hours earlier, there can be roads that opened after the updated was finished, roads closed for repairs, and roads that are impassable due to flooding, rock slides, or other problems. Maybe the GPS can re-route you, maybe it can't.

The biggest step to being safe if you are lost is to memorize addresses and phone numbers (home and cell) for your immediate family (parents, siblings), grandparents, and anyone else you trust who is nearby. Sometimes a friend is the best person to call, if they obsessively check their phone for messages. Sometimes a grandparent is the best choice, if they rarely leave home and always pick up quickly. Take a few minutes to think it through and memorize those phone numbers because just as a cell phone signal can be lost, so can a phone and phone batteries can die, leaving you without your contacts list.

Asking for Help

A common piece of advice is to find a police officer and ask them for help. The problem with that is sometimes there are people who look like police but are really just security guards with little or no training. Most of them are nice enough guys, but not all are. If you see someone and are sure they are really a police officer (someone in a patrol car, for example), that's OK, but there is another choice, and it's someone far easier to find: Ask a mom for help. A mom with kids will usually make sure you get help. She may stick with you, if she can, until your family actually arrives, and annoy you by being a mom and hovering, or she may have to leave quickly to take care of her own family, but there is very little chance that she will ignore your problem. If you get that very, very rare mean mom who blows you off, there is a probably another mom, or grandma, nearby you can ask for help. Moms are not in short supply in the world.

If you ask someone for help and they want you to leave and go with them somewhere, that's a bad idea, unless you really are in the middle of nowhere or an otherwise dangerous location. Stay close to where your family last saw you to make it easier to be found, and if you have to go elsewhere, leave a note so they know where to look.

At an Event/Activity

When you arrive, set up a specific place and time to meet if you get lost. If you do get lost and can't find your way back, ask someone, like a police officer or a parent with a child, to help you get back there. If you didn't set up a meeting place, ask for help and remember not to leave the area. The farther you wander from where you are supposed to be, the harder it is for anyone looking for you to find you. Know where family and friends live in case you need to find them.

Stay in One Place

The farther you wander from where you are supposed to be, the harder it is for anyone looking for you to find you. I followed my son in a parade. His Boy Scout Troop was just ahead of the Cub Scout Pack I was with. The Pack stopped in front of an old school and the Troop continued walking behind the building. I waited, expecting him to come out. After about 15 minutes, I followed the same path he did. Naturally, the Troop leaders dismissed them and I just missed seeing them come around the front. By the time I walked the entire school, he was gone, out of sight down the street. He didn't have a phone and kept walking back the parade route toward the beginning. Since I had no idea where he was headed, I had to check all the little stores and vendors he could have been sidetracked into visiting. By the time he had a friend call, it was over half an hour later.

If I had continued waiting in front of the building, I would have seen him come out. If he had walked to the front of the school and stopped, I would have seen him. If he had stopped and watched for me at any point in the parade route, I would have seen him. But I moved to find, and he never stopped to wait for me.

Epic fail.

If you are lost, or simply can't find the person you are supposed to meet, stop moving. Stay where you are, or go back to where you were to meet, and stay there.

While Traveling in a Car

In most cases, leaving the car and going cross-country (away from the road) is a Very Bad Idea. Not a peak-at-your-gifts-early-bad idea. A wreck-the-car-through-the-house-and-into-the-pool-with-all-the-relatives-visiting-bad idea. A car near a road is easier to find than a single person wandering, with no idea where they might be. If anyone knew where you were headed, even generally, staying near the road keeps you closer to the route where they will look for you. (Most of us use one of a few systems to map our trips now, so entering in start and end data will give an extremely good idea of your route.)

One of the biggest times people get stuck and decide to go cross-country seems to be during snowstorms. On a normal road in a normal snow storm, road crews will clear the road within a day or two, well within the range when it is safer to stay. Most roads will have crews cleaning them within a few hours.

The one big *huge* exception to that is if, for some unknown reason, you and your vehicle are on a closed road, help won't be coming. The same is often true if you are on a private road, unless someone has paid a maintenance crew to plow it after every snowfall. There are also situations where people get stuck in the middle of nowhere and there either isn't a road or the road is the (much) longer route, so the best choice is (or seems to be) to ignore the roads and go cross-country. Staying on the road is still normally the best choice because it's so much easier to find you that way.

Activity

Memorize the phone numbers for your parents, siblings, and anyone else you might need to contact in an emergency, most particularly personal cell phone numbers. (Some people also have work cell phone numbers but people seem to be more likely to carry their personal cell phone, but you should know the habits of those you are closest to.)

Quick Quiz

T/F   Moms are often good people to ask for help, even if they are strangers.

T/F   If you are lost, keep moving. Never stop and wait for help.

T/F   If you are stuck in your car, always leave to search for help.

T/F   Leaving with strangers is a good idea.

T/F   Police officers can help when you are lost.

Resources

Articles

Essential Safety for Kids: If A Child Gets Lost (elementary)
www.netmums.com/lifestyle/house-and-home/essential-safety-for-kids/essential-safety-for-kids-if-a-child-gets-lost

Lost in the Wilderness? Experts Share Tips on Staying Safe
www.pe.com/2018/01/16/lost-in-the-wilderness-experts-share-tips-on-staying-safe/

Staying Safe Outdoors
www.fs.fed.us/recreation/safety/safety.shtml

What if I Get Lost?
www.kidpower.org/library/article/getting-lost/

Scouting-Specific

Search and Rescue Merit Badge
meritbadge.org/wiki/index.php/Search_%26_Rescue

{PART 5}
ESCAPE AND EVASION

If Something Bad happens and you are caught up in the middle of it, escape and evasion become very important. Escape is getting away from the danger entirely. Evasion is avoiding it when you are very close to, or even surrounded by, the danger.

Camouflage, Concealment, and Cover: Camouflage is when you do something to blend in. The first thing that comes to mind is the fabric patterns worn by hunters and the military that are designed to blend into the woods and other backgrounds. In some neighborhoods, a hoody with baggy jeans would be effective camouflage. In others, a business suit might make you effectively invisible. It all depends on what everyone else is wearing.

Concealment is being hidden from view. Cover is being protected from injury. A blanket will almost always conceal a person, but it doesn't provide cover because it doesn't protect from injury.

Hiding and Trap Points: Hiding is almost the same as concealment, except it is potentially for a longer time and may be in a larger space. Trap points are places where it is easy to become trapped.

Urban Dangers and Resources: Parks, dumpsters, abandoned homes and vehicles, schools.... The list of places that may have resources you can use in a true disaster is immense. Rats, feral (wild) animals, gangs, crazy drivers, polluted water.... Again, the list of potential dangers is very long.

Answering Questions: Most people never have to go through a true interrogation, but you could have a less-intense questioning you need to be able to handle if Something Bad has just happened.

{TWENTY}

CAMOUFLAGE, COVER, AND

CONCEALMENT

Escape and evasion is always easiest if they can't find you to begin with, and you certainly don't want them to see you escaping and evading. So how to achieve this? **Camouflage is the art of blending in so that no one notices you.** In some situations, being invisible (or at least not noticeable) is the safest possible choice. Other times, we need to be entirely hidden to stay safe, which is where cover and concealment come into play. **Cover and concealment are the arts of hiding and not being noticed. Concealment keeps you from being seen. Cover keeps you safe(r).**

It is important to remember that sometimes it's important to be visible, even highly visible. That's why hunters wear bright orange, traffic cops have brightly colored vests, and reflective tape is sold in fabric stores. The techniques in this chapter aren't necessary in everyday life. They are primarily for emergencies where other people are the main danger. In some emergencies, you want other people to find you, so you want to wear bright colors to stand out.

Camouflage

You may still be seen—you may be in plain sight—but if you aren't noticed, it doesn't matter. The most famous kind of camouflage is, of course, worn by the military and hunters to blend into the woods. Another kind of camouflage popular in movies and pop culture takes the face paint used by the military to an unbelievable level. Even when people look directly at them, in plain sight, they may be effectively invisible because of how well they blend in to the background. Sometimes, people are overlooked because of ingrained habits and biases. Service workers (janitors, cooks, security) are often overlooked, even by people who are looking straight at them. That's why it's such a movie stereotype to have spies pretend to be in those jobs.

Ironically, camouflage that perfectly conceals you in one environment can make you stand out like zebra in the middle of a herd of sheep in another. When your surroundings change, your camouflage must change as well. Wearing an expensive suit on Wall Street will help you blend in as surely as swimsuit blends in at the beach, but can you even imagine reversing the outfits? Talk about standing out!

Outside

The green and brown woodland camouflage long favored by the military and hunters is what most people think of when they talk about "camouflage." Camouflage (or "camo") fabric patterns actually come in a wide variety of colors and styles to accommodate a wide variety of environments. Blues (water), tans (desert), grays (urban), and gray and white (snow/Arctic) are the most common. There are also specialized camouflage items for hunting, such as ghillie suits, and digitized patterns. Of course, each color comes in a variety of patterns since each manufacturer has slightly different patterns and different areas have different flora and fauna, and there are "fun camo" patterns that don't blend into anything, such a pink camo. Of course, not all "outside" is in the woods or nature. If you are in a city, "camouflage" usually means dressing and acting like all the people around you so you blend in, like the example with Wall Street and the beach.

Hunting and the outdoors are not the only places camouflage comes in handy. Anytime a person needs to blend in, camouflage is in order. The big difference is that outdoors, you are probably doing something (clothing, make-up, ghillie suit) to blend into your surroundings/nature. Inside you almost always need to blend into a group of people so you are not noticed.

Inside

Hunting and the outdoors are not the only places camouflage comes in handy. Anytime a person needs to blend in, camouflage is in order. The big difference is that outdoors, you are probably actively working to blend into your surroundings/nature with clothing, make-up, ghillie suits, etc. Inside you almost always need to blend into a group of people so you are not noticed. Concealment and cover are usually bigger priorities than camouflage inside.

Concealment vs. Cover

Concealment keeps you from being seen. Cover keeps you safe.

Even though concealment keeps others from seeing you, that doesn't mean you can't be injured. Imagine a movie scene where people are hiding behind furniture and regular walls. The bad guys come in and start shooting everything with their magical, never-runs-out-of-ammo weapons, or an earthquake hits and the building collapses. In either case, the people were hidden, or concealed, but were still injured.

On the other hand, if those same people were under a steel desk, their odds of survival would have been much, *much* higher because they had *cover*, not just *concealment*.

How Long?

Hopefully, help will be there or the danger will leave within just a few minutes, but there is no way to know in advance.

When and Why?

Sometimes, it's just not safe to be seen. Other times, escaping is critical, but it's not possible yet so hiding buys time until you can escape.

Finding Shelter

Convenience stores are the first places most people think of for shelter and are often targets for petty thieves. They also seem to be the first places rioters and looters hit. As such, they aren't a great choice for safe shelter in an emergency. Neighborhood markets are a better choice, but still not great because they get hit right after convenience and electronics stores. They typically have a smallish selection of food and drinks. If there is a store selling cheap junk people don't need, that should be your first choice for shelter because it probably won't be the looters' and rioters' first choice.

As noted above, gangs tend to be in poor neighborhoods and are rarely in rich ones, but poor doesn't automatically mean dangerous any more than rich automatically means safe. If you are caught in a strange area and are looking for a safe place, you need to look thoughtfully at the area, especially the people, not just at how expensive the buildings seem to be. Much like feral animals, people who look or act aggressive or scared are likely to be more dangerous and unpredictable, and there is no correlation between how much money a person has in their bank account and how they act, especially in an emergency.

Any neighborhood where the doors and windows are covered by bars, gates, fences, or guards of any sort is likely, but far from guaranteed, to be suspicious. On the other hand, if violence is common, the locals can almost certainly tell the difference between human predators and prey and may be willing to help you escape the predators. Some fear and defensiveness is unavoidable in an emergency, but try to find a place where you see other emotions, not just fear and anger, especially toward strangers.

When you go up to a building seeking shelter, knock on the door, then step back a few steps so you aren't crowding the door and the occupant can see you through their peephole, if they have one. Hold up your hands to show you aren't holding any weapons and be as non-threatening as possible when you ask for help. If they say no, it's OK to ask again but under no circumstance should you do anything that can be perceived as threatening, including yelling at them. (If it's so noisy they can't hear you unless you yell, then it's okay.)

Areas with very little light make it easier for bad guys to attack you and easier for good guys to mistake you for a bad guy trying to attack them, so try to stay in well-lit areas. In the end, though, you may simply need to find a small space you can fit into and hide there until you can leave and walk somewhere else safely.

Hiding

Sometimes, the best choice is to simply hide until the danger passes, or at least moves far enough away for you to have a chance to reach safety. **It is important to remember not to hide without telling the others you are with (especially adults and little kids) where you are hiding unless stopping to tell them could be a fatal mistake.**

Hiding is different from camouflage because with camouflage, you may still be visible, but you aren't noticeable. Woodland camouflage makes it harder to see a person in the woods compared to a pair of blue jeans and a white t-shirt. In the middle of a library, neither one is going to make it harder to see you. Hiding in a closet, behind the circulation desk, keeps you entirely out of sight. (If it doesn't, then you aren't hidden.)

Depending on the situation and the size of your hiding spot, you may be able to help others hide as well. When terrorists attacked a music hall in Paris, two friends successfully hid in the basement. They probably could have shared it with others if they had arrived at the same time, but then they had to shut the door to stay safe, even when they heard others in trouble outside. If they had opened the door, they probably would have died as well. In other instances, someone hidden has been able to grab others and pull them into a safe spot. It entirely depends on the situation, but if you are caught because you are trying to help someone else at the wrong time, that isn't ultimately a help to anyone.

Activity

For one day, look around every place you visit, including your home, school, and after school activities, for places that offer concealment, then look for cover. Think about what would be effective camouflage. Discuss what you found with your parent or guardian

Quick Quiz

T/F   Concealment provides more protection than cover.

T/F   You always need cover; concealment is never enough.

T/F   For hide and seek, you need concealment.

T/F   Before hiding, always tell those with you where you plan to hide unless it is a true life or death situation and you don't have time.

T/F   Stay with or near your friends and family when you hide, if at all possible.

Resources

Articles

Artist paints himself to blend into background
holykaw.alltop.com/artist-paints-himself-to-blend-into-backgroun

Urban Camouflage: Why You Should Blend in To Walk Home After a Disaster
survivalcommonsense.com/dress-for-urban-disaster/

Books

Appear to Vanish: Stealth Concepts for Effective Camouflage and Concealment by Matthew Dermody

*Gray Man: Camouflage for Crowds, Cities, and Civil Crisis by Matthew Dermody

Videos

Escape and Evasion: Camouflage, Cover, and Concealment
www.youtube.com/watch?v=WEMs1Qq1omg

*Former CIA Chief of Disguise Breaks Down 30 Spy Scenes From Fil & TV
www.youtube.com/watch?v=mUqeBMP8nEg

Former CIA Operative Explains How Spies Use Disguises
www.youtube.com/watch?v=JASUsVY5YJ8

Tim Kennedy Explains How to Dress | Sheepdog Response
www.youtube.com/watch?v=GYjE6nDmjb0

{TWENTY-ONE}

HIDING AND TRAP POINTS

T rap points are what it sounds like: places it is easy to become trapped. It is far easier to become trapped in a vehicle than on foot. Vehicles require a lot more space, and firmer ground, to maneuver. People can duck into a building and hide in a bathroom. Good luck trying that with a sub-compact car, much less an SUV or mini-van!

If something bad happens, being aware of what is and has recently been around you could make the difference between safety and danger because safe points can turn into trap points. The denser things are (buildings, trees, traffic, anything), the more places there are to hide, but the more places there are to be trapped. Keeping aware of your surroundings is an important first step for both hiding and avoiding trap points. Thinking ahead and having a plan is another important step.

- On a rainy day, noticing that water is nearly flowing over a bridge might inspire you to find a safer way to drive or walk back later, when it may start flooding.
- Noticing a road crew preparing to rip up a road may save delays returning home.
- Trap points are good places to set up ambushes.

- Trap points are also good places to control access to your location. If there is one near your home or safe place, use it to your advantage.

If you have been paying attention, you should have enough notice to duck out of the way and hide from any danger before it gets near you. It is possible to stay safe, even in a trap point, if you are hidden well enough. If you have learned how to use camouflage, concealment, and cover, and to pay attention to your surroundings, that will go far in keeping you safe, even if you end up stuck because of a trap point.

Alleys

Alleys are small. Some are short and almost immediately end in a building, but others stretch for miles through cities, bypassing busier main roads and running behind hundreds of houses. Either way, they are narrower than more major streets. Alleys that end almost immediately (the kind beloved of TV crime shows) are clearly trap points. What about the other kind? It depends. Look at them. I have seen long alleys in cities that run between two main streets. Their primary purpose is to allow access to the garages behind the homes on those main streets. The alleys could be empty, unwatched, and the safest route out. They could also be completely filled with a line of slow-moving cars trying to escape, or with scared homeowners afraid of looters trying to get in their back door, and you might just look like a looter to them.

Alleys in another city I visited were overgrown with plants from backyard gardens. On foot, in particular, those lovely plants and garden gates provide a fantastic place for Bad People to hide and grab you. Or, conversely, for you to hide from Bad People.

Buildings

It is possible to become trapped inside a building in an emergency. The building might be the safest place near you, but it will not be someplace you can stay permanently. If nothing else, you will eventually run out of supplies in a long emergency, even if the building is a giant warehouse store. Most buildings have more than one floor. In an emergency, the highest floors (anything over seven) are almost never a good place to be, so try to get to a lower floor as soon as it is safe to do so. Use the stairs to get there because elevators can be a trap point, especially if the power goes out.

If you are caught in a building and need firefighters to help you get out, they will probably use one of two tools. One is a simple ladder put against the side of the building. This is easy to set up and move, and doesn't take much space. The other is a ladder on a ladder truck. The longest ladder truck ladders used in the USA are around 100 feet fully extended, and many companies have shorter ladders. That does not mean 100 feet straight up in the air, though, because trucks wouldn't normally be parked right up against a building for safety reasons, including the safety of firefights working near the building. The maximum floor a fire truck ladder could reach is the tenth floor. If you plan to stay in a building, your goal should be to be absolutely no higher than the tenth floor, preferably not higher than the seventh, and hopefully closer to the third or fourth floor. Just because there are trucks that can reach the tenth floor doesn't mean one is available near you right when you need it.

If you are on the first or second floor, it is easier for someone outside to see you. If you think they will rescue and help you, then move to the first or second floor. If you think they are more likely to be dangerous, stay on the third floor. Either way, make sure you know at least two ways to exit the building quickly if you need to. If there is only one way, that is a trap point.

Crowd/Mob

The biggest difference between a crowd and a mob is that a mob is a crowd that has gotten wound up and angry. Sometimes, there is an event we want to go to that will have large crowds at it. Conventions, competitions, and other gatherings with people who are all interested in the same thing can all be a lot of fun to go to and are perfectly safe. Crowds are generally safe and rarely turn into mobs, but they can turn into mobs fairly quickly, if something happens or someone does something to make them angry. Mobs move together as one unit and members of the mob will do things that the individuals would not normally do. Mobs are dangerous to themselves and those around them.

The kind of crowds that seem the most likely to be turned into a mob are the ones that gathered for a cause, especially there is anger related to that cause. They already believe something is being done wrong and want to have it fixed. It is unlikely that they want to do anything more dangerous than march or yell about their feelings, but that can change. One person standing up and giving a radical speech can push a peaceful crowd toward being a mob. Once a mob forms, it is extremely difficult to talk it back down to being a crowd. A mob creates something called "mob mentality." Individual people within the mob stop feeling responsible for their own actions and let the larger group dictate what they do; reason and normal standards of behavior stop applying. When a large group of people, most of whom do not feel responsible for their actions, do something, it is rarely good.

As emotions begin to wane, the mob mentality will as well and the mob itself will start to disperse. With luck, that happens before they do anything more than say ugly, threatening things. As that happens, the individual people will begin to realize what they have and done and respond, emotionally, to that. Some may feel guilt or anger. It is not safe to confront people who are or recently have been part of a mob.

If you see a crowd that seems like it could form a mob, look around for potential trap points and hiding places. If you can't leave the area entirely, move toward a potential hiding place, but don't actually hide unless you need to. And remember: don't hide without telling the people you are with where to find you.

Elevators

If you are in an elevator and it gets stuck, how can you get out?

1. Push the "door open" button. If you are at a landing and there is power, the door may simply open and you are on your merry way. Take the steps the rest of the way to your final destination.

2. Push the "close door" button in case it's stuck, then try "door open" again.

3. Push the red "Emergency" call button and talk to whoever answers.

4. Bang on the door and see if anyone hears you. Ask for help.

5. Call for help. The elevator may have a telephone in it, but either you or someone with you almost certainly does. Use it.

Trying to force the doors open or get out through an emergency hatch on the roof are also options, but they aren't good ones in anything except a dire emergency. If the elevator stopped because an earthquake hit the building and the elevator is now at an angle, going through that ceiling hatch or prying open the doors (if you have the raw strength) are options, but you still need to use care so you don't jump from the frying pan into the fire, so to speak. They are great options if you happen to be James Bond. For the rest of us, the reality is that an elevator repair tech will almost certainly arrive within an hour, probably much sooner, and have you safely out and on your way without any property damage or physical injury. Forcing open the elevator doors or ceiling hatch could definitely result in thousands of dollars of property damage and should not be done except in a true emergency. Yes, I know that is repetitive but it bears repeating.

If a natural disaster has just come through, emergency crews will be busy already and any additional property damage to the building won't be noticed. If not, then it's fairly clear which damage was from a freaked-out passenger, who can expect to receive a bill for the damages. This will *not* please anyone.

The even bigger reason for not forcing doors open and then crawling through the small gap is that the doors could snap shut or the elevator could start moving again, with a person half in and half out. The end result is serious injury or, more likely, death. Similarly, a person who has crawled out the ceiling hatch onto the elevator roof could either fall off the side or be crushed if the elevator starts moving while they are outside of the car. In addition, elevators have two sets of doors (an inside set that moves with the elevator and an outside set that stays with the floor) that must be pried open. Neither one is easy to open, so *a lot* of strength is required.

<u>Simply staying inside the nice metal box is almost always the safest option, even if it does get boring.</u>

Natural Boundaries

Natural boundaries are permanent, natural borders that are difficult to cross. Cliffs, canyons, mountains, rivers, oceans–natural boundaries come in many forms. Since they cannot easily be crossed, particularly with a vehicle, they can are often trap points. Other normally passable areas can become trap points. Many roads are surrounded by woods or cross over streams. If trees fall or are cut down, blocking the road, they have created a new trap point. Likewise, a normally passable road could be blocked by an avalanche, mudslide, flood or rockslide.

Some natural boundaries are set, such as rivers and oceans, but water falls down from the sky in often unpredictable ways. Heavy rainfall can lead to storm surges, mudslides, and flash floods. Steady rain can lead to rivers, lakes, and ponds flooding. Heavy snows can lead to avalanches, roof collapses, and white-outs. (A white-out is when there is so much snow it's impossible to see.) When the snow melts, it can lead to mudslides and flash floods. Storm surges, mudslides, and flash floods are just a few more ways Mother Nature can create new or temporary trap points.

There are also artificial or man-made borders. Some of these are the walls, guard posts, and security features associated with political borders between countries, but the gates and fences that surround gated communities and farms are also man-made borders, of a sort.

Traffic

There are multiple ways to become stuck in traffic. Gridlock on city streets and massive slow-downs (even stops) on highways are the two most common. Accidents, construction, and squeeze-downs (where the number of lanes going in a certain direction decreases) cause delays, but not usually outright stoppages, at least not for long.

City streets form a grid of streets going different directions. Vehicles turn or go straight at intersections at every block, and most are four-way stops. In true grid-lock, something has happened so that none of the vehicles are able to move. The light turns green, but the vehicles on the other side of the intersection haven't moved since the last time it turned green. No new cars can go through. Normal rush hour often provokes a modified form of this where only a few cars get through per light cycle.

Gridlock is fairly predictable. Any time a large number of people need to drive in the city at the same time, expect moderate to severe gridlock. In an emergency, either get out early, or wait until the gridlock clears. There are better ways to use your time and your fuel. (Sitting in traffic uses precious fuel even if you aren't moving much, or at all, unless the car is turned off.)

On the very rare occasions when a highway is so fully stopped that people get out of their cars and walk around on the road, it is almost always caused by a massive accident of some sort. It could be a natural accident such as a rock fall. This is harder to predict than gridlock, but in a true emergency, the odds are higher than usual that some stressed out or distracted driver will make a mistake and cause just such a massive accident. Smaller roads and side streets, even alleys, are usually the best and fastest choice in a true emergency, wherever trap points such as bridges, tunnels, or mountains don't make that impossible.

Activity

Look around one place you visit often (family, friends, sports field, church, whatever) and notice the possible trap points both there and on the way there. Figure out ways to avoid them and to escape from them if you get caught there.

Quick Quiz

T/F   Something either is or is not a trap point. A safe area can't change to become a trap point.

T/F   Climbing out the roof hatch is always the best choice if you are stuck in an elevator

T/F   Trap points are places that can become dangerous.

T/F   People can create trap points.

T/F   Weather, such as heavy rain, can create new trap points.

Resources

Articles

Active Shooter
www.ready.gov/active-shooter

During an Emergency
www.getprepared.gc.ca/cnt/hzd/drng-en.aspx

How high can the fire department's highest ladder reach?
www.waukeshanow.com/news/wkn_col_nyk_ladder_1215art-523dk3f-135531148.html

How to Escape a High Rise Building During an Emergency
www.realworldsurvivor.com/2018/11/28/how-to-escape-a-high-rise-building-during-an-emergency/

Know the Difference: Shelter in Place and Lockdown
www.army.mil/article/184872/know_the_difference_shelter_in_place_and_lockdown_2_very_different_emergency_responses

What are Artificial Borders?
www.lifepersona.com/what-are-artificial-borders-features-and-types

Books

The Story in My Father's Footlockers: A WWII Story of Escape, Evasion and Unexpected Friendships by Juliann K. Pendolino

Survive Like a Spy: Real CIA Operatives Reveal How They Stay Safe in a Dangerous World and How You Can Too by Jason Hanson

Videos

Bourne Fire Aerial Fire Truck
www.youtube.com/watch?v=0AVjZ3gxnTo

Tim Kennedy Explains the Levels of Situational Awareness | Sheepdog Response
https://www.youtube.com/watch?v=GYjE6nDmjb0

{TWENTY-TWO}

URBAN DANGERS AND RESOURCES

I f you live in a city, you probably already know how to avoid these. If you are only in popular tourist spots, they aren't likely to be a big problem because city police know where tourists spend most of their time and keep those areas as safe as possible because they need the tourist revenue. However, in an emergency you might end up going to areas you wouldn't normally, whether you live there or are just visiting.

This chapter was very uncomfortable for me to write because, by its nature, it includes some fairly sweeping generalizations about areas that are safe and unsafe. These are meant to help readers find safety quickly in an emergency situation, nothing more. It's important to remember that safe and unsafe areas can be very close. It's not unusual for dangerous neighborhoods to be only a few blocks from highly patrolled, safe tourist areas.

Alleys

Alleys are narrow, cramped, often twisty, poorly lit, and neither cars nor people spend much time in them. As discussed in Chapter 21 on Trap Points, alleys can be a trap point. On a bright, broad avenue, it is usually easy to stay away from areas where desperate people can literally grab you. The much smaller size and poor lighting in alleys make it all too easy for desperate people to hide and grab you or your belongings when you venture too near. The lack of both pedestrians and cars makes it unlikely someone will hear or see you and come to your aid. They can be a breeding ground for all kinds of crime. They can also be a quick route away from danger, so listen to your intuition and common sense, and to those with you.

This is even truer in an emergency. In some areas, there are long alleys that run behind buildings to allow parking and access. They function almost like single lane streets. In an emergency, these will probably have a lot more people in them than on a normal day, but that doesn't mean they will notice or help you. They are probably busy with their own problems. In other areas, alleys are much shorter, merely providing side access to or emergency egress from the buildings on either side. These alleys are a place you can try to hide for a short time, but with only the one way out (assuming you can't get into the buildings), they are also a trap point. In a large-scale upheaval like a riot, the masses of people are likely to spill into alleyways that function like streets as they make their way around. Some may spill into the smaller ones that don't connect to anywhere, but most won't. The few who do are unlikely to move very far back, where it is darker and generally more dangerous, and will probably leave quickly.

The biggest reason alleys pose a danger is because all of the other dangers discussed in this chapter can hide in alleys, to greater or lesser degrees. Feral dogs and rats are particularly likely to hide in alleys where they can find food in garbage cans, dumpsters, or even just on the ground.

Crazy People

The truth is that most of crazy-looking (often homeless) people in cities are addicts (alcohol or drugs) or mentally ill, but that doesn't make them an actual danger to you. That doesn't make approaching strangers safe because you don't really know which ones are safe and which aren't, but it does mean you shouldn't freak out if you see a dirty, disheveled stranger panhandling, or even if one walks up asking for money, but I know I would try to keep my distance, especially if the situation is already dangerous. All you need to do is look at pictures of San Francisco's streets from around 2020 to see the dangers discarded needles and other blight caused by homeless can cause. Use your common sense, instincts, and situational awareness to size up the situation.

With that said, anyone brandishing a weapon is obviously a threat and should be avoided, as are gangs. Anyone who looks ill is best avoided as well, simply to stay healthy. Personally, I avoid anyone who clearly seems to be psychotic. That means they are having hallucinations and cannot tell what is real and what is not real. Their hallucinations may cause them to do something unexpected and dangerous. I know a young girl whose psychosis led her to run into traffic. She was trying to save another person, but the person wasn't real.

The easiest way to avoid gangs is to stay in touristy areas. Simply put, most gangs have a defined territory confine most of their activities to this territory. Cities are highly intolerant of any gang claiming a tourist area as part of their territory because they need the income from tourists. Rich neighborhoods are also generally able to keep gangs out. It's a broad generalization, but if you stay in tourist areas or richer neighborhoods, you are less likely to run into gangs.

With that said, poor, gang-riddled neighborhoods can be shockingly close to tourist areas, college campuses, and other places you may visit. Pay attention to where you are going–and make sure your phone has a working GPS app! If buildings start looking abandoned, the streets are deserted, or people on the street seem threatening, turn around and go back to where you started. If nothing else, it will be hard to find help if the area is effectively abandoned. If it is truly a life-or-death situation and you can't go back, try to find a small store you can shelter in until you find your way to safety.

Food and Water

Ponds and other water features in parks are the most obvious sources of water, followed by water fountains (the decorative kind). Two harder-to-access options are fire hydrants and exterior hose hook-ups (sillcocks) on most large buildings. Almost none of this water is actually potable, so take the time to review the steps in making water potable and using a water filter in *26 Basic Life Skills*. Sillcocks on commercial buildings can generally be opened using an inexpensive gadget called a sillcock key.

In even a few days, grocery store shelves are quickly picked bare. They rely on a constant stream of new inventory and in a disaster, those trucks stop arriving. Add customers who are suddenly buying more and the problem is easy to see. If you are stuck in a city with a disaster headed your way, the smart thing to do is buy enough non-perishable food to last you or your group for at least a few days. Depending on the nature of the emergency, you may have a working microwave, hot water, and refrigerator, or no power at all.

Rats

Rats are just part of cities, and they always have been. All the people in cities generate a lot of trash, and some of that trash is food waste. The trash attracts rats. Rats will eat anything they can, including (in very rare instances) people, so garbage dumpsters are a real feast for them. They can even chew through concrete, metal, and plastic. Clearly, they have strong teeth. They will not hesitate to use these to bite anything that threatens them, and they carry diseases. Lots of diseases. They also carry fleas and mites that spread more diseases. As one example, the spread of the Black Death was blamed, in part, on rats.

Like many wild animals, a healthy rat is more likely to flee than attack if a person stumbles upon it. The problem is that "more likely" isn't a guarantee. If you encounter a wild rat, move away from it without doing anything to threaten it. Its nest may be nearby, possibly even its babies, and the protectiveness of mothers is legendary. It could also be sick, and sick rats are both more likely to attack and more dangerous because of the risk of passing on diseases. If you can't avoid rats and are bitten by one, seek medical attention as soon as possible. If you kill or capture the rat that bit you, bring it so it can be examined to see what diseases, if any, you are at risk for from the bite.

Sewage

No one really wants to mess around with sewage, which is why people who work with it have to be well paid. In cities, the sewage system takes it all away, but that assumes it is working and people use it (Septic systems are common in rural areas and are only connected to one property.) Homeless and drunk people often pee in alleys and other public areas. Again, look at images of San Francisco homeless around 2020.

In an emergency, the sewage system may stop working. In extreme circumstances, you could find yourself forced into underground tunnels, which may include the main lines for sewage and water runoff tunnels. In periods of heavy flooding or high runoff, these sewage main lines can overfill and overflow. These means the streets will literally be running with sewage. Earthquakes and other disasters can cause them to crack or rupture entirely. This is arguably one of the biggest public health risks in the aftermath of a disaster.

If you are confronted with sewage, the precautions are fairly obvious. Don't eat or drink anything that has come in contact with it. Avoid touching it, especially with your skin. Be vigilant about keeping any cuts or sores away from sewage. If they do touch, clean yourself thoroughly as soon as possible and use some kind of anti-bacterial. Even though it hurts, this is a good time to use alcohol to help ensure all the germs and bacteria are dead. Don't let anything contaminated by sewage near your eyes, nose, or mouth. Use a solution of bleach and water to kill germs and bacteria on clothing and other cleanable objects.

Short version: Avoid sewage. If you're near it, don't touch it. If you somehow touched it, clean up as soon as possible and don't spread the contamination any further by touching other things. Clean whatever was contaminated ASAP. Do not to let germs past the protection of your skin through either injuries (cuts, abrasions) or orifices (eyes, nose, mouth).

Wild (Feral) Dogs

Dogs are descended from wolves, and feral (wild) dogs run in packs, just like wolves. No matter how much they may look like a pet, they aren't. They may bite you and may have diseases, including rabies. Don't underestimate them. They are true predators. A pack of wild dogs can kill a human. A pack can even kill an armed human for the simple reason that there are more of them. Even if one or two are shot, they can overwhelm a single person before they can reload, or knock them down so they lose their gun.

Predators prefer not to be seen, and feral dogs are predators. They prefer dusk, night, and dawn–times with low light. Since they travel in packs, they normally have a den where they relax and sleep. Depending on the pack size and other factors, there may be a clear path to it and there may be other signs of habitation, like piles of bones, food debris, and even poop. Steer clear of these areas.

If a dog is snapping, biting, growling, has raised fur, or is generally acting aggressively, heed the warning and stay away. Other danger signs include drooling and limping, which could be signs of disease or injury. Imagine how scary it is for a human to be sick or injured; now imagine what it's like for an animal that can't understand what is happening. It won't know you are trying to help and your actions may look downright threatening, so just leave it alone.

If you are already within attack range, put some kind of barrier between you. Do not use this to attack the dog! The goal is defense, not offense. Something as simple as a snowboard can help block an attack. Remember that running or moving quickly may be interpreted as a threat and provoke an attack by any wild animal. When meeting a pet, the most common thing to do is to put out a hand for it to sniff. Don't do this with a wild animal! Once again, it may be interpreted as a threat and lead to being bitten.

Feral dogs may approach and sniff people. The best response is to simply stand still until it moves away, but don't look it in the eye. This is a challenge for any wild animal. When it is safe, walk slowly away, but don't turn your back on a wild animal. It might still attack. In fact, it might attack even when you are a distance away. Dogs can run faster than humans.

If you are bitten, try to take a picture of the animal and definitely make a note of the location. If it has a collar or any identifying marks, write these down right away, before you forget them. This will help authorities/animal control if they need to track down the animal to check it for disease. Also take pictures of your injuries. If your clothing is ripped or damaged, bag it (unwashed) and keep it. All of this will help if you ever need evidence of what happened. If someone calls and asks you questions, don't answer them unless an adult says it's okay. (They might be trying to get you to say something so they, and their insurance, don't have to pay medical and other related expenses.)

If you see one or more feral or injured animals, dogs or otherwise, that you think need help, don't approach them yourself. The best thing to do is to call animal control. It's their job to handle wild animals of all sorts. They have the training, tools, and facilities to do so safely.

Activity

Watch the videos and compare the neighborhoods

Quick Quiz

T/F   All alleys have dead ends.

T/F   It's easy and safe to make friends with feral dogs.

T/F   Convenience stores are the best place to seek shelter.

T/F   Rats carry disease. So does sewage.

T/F   If you have the right gadget, you can get potable water from the outside of some commercial buildings.

Resources

Articles

Cleaning up After Flood and Sewer Overflows
dph.illinois.gov/topics-services/environmental-health-protection/toxicology/indoor-air-quality-healthy-homes/flood-sewer-overflow-cleanup

Giant Rat Crawls on Sleeping NYC Subway Rider
www.opposingviews.com/i/society/horrified-subway-riders-pulled-out-their-phones-proof-minute-they-realized-what-was-right

How to Protect Yourself Against Dangerous Stray Dogs
www.wildlifeanimalcontrol.com/straydogprotect.html

How to Survive a Feral Dog Attack
survivethecomingcollapse.com/2605/how-to-survive-a-feral-dog-attack/

New York's Looming Food Disaster
www.citylab.com/politics/2013/10/new-yorks-looming-food-disaster/7294/

Staying Safe When You Live in a Bad Neighborhood
www.safewise.com/blog/staying-safe-when-you-live-in-a-bad-neighborhood/

Top 10 Health Risks of Sewage Damage Exposure
www.examiner.com/article/top-10-health-risks-of-sewage-damage-exposure

What should I do if I've been bitten by a stray dog?
www.wildlifeanimalcontrol.com/straydogbite.html

Books

Escape the Wolf: A Security Handbook for Traveling Professionals by Clinton Emerson

Hidden in Plain Sight: A Prepper's Guide to Hiding, Discovering, and Scavenging Diversion Safes and Caches by Matthew Dermody

SAS Urban Survival Handbook by John "Lofty" Wiseman

Street Survival Skills: Tips, Tricks and Tactics for Modern Survival by Fernando "Ferfal" Aquirre

Other

Sillcock Key
smile.amazon.com/dp/B0002YVMEM/

Scouting-Specific

Public Health Merit Badge
meritbadge.org/wiki/index.php/Public_Health

Videos

Awareness of Your Urban Surroundings
www.youtube.com/watch?v=4lS5HRmcznE

How to Handle High Stress Environments | 5 Tips Prepare For Stressful Environments | Military
www.youtube.com/watch?v=oRLt7h0yXY8

The Importance of Being Aware of Your Surroundings
patch.com/massachusetts/natick/bp--the-importance-of-being-aware-of-your-surroundings

{Twenty-Three}

Answering Questions

Most of us will never have to go through a true interrogation, but most of us do have to go through being questioned in life. This starts with our parents when we are toddlers and continues until we die, especially if we die of old age. Old people end up getting asked a lot of questions, many of them designed to see how their memory and health are holding up. There is a wide range from the well-meant questioning of our loving family to the ministrations of organizations like the KGB and Gestapo. Some are easy to handle. Some involve literal torture and potentially even death. You are not likely to encounter torture and death as a result of questioning. Whenever you feel like an authority figure in your life (parent, teacher, police officer, boss) is being too forceful in their questioning, remember that they aren't a secret police force authorized to do anything they want with no repercussions.

ANSWERING QUESTIONS

Simple Questions

This is the most common experience. Someone simply wants information from you. Often, it is due to curiosity but they might also need it for some reason. It is easiest to simply give them complete, truthful answers. That might be a single word–yes, no, Hawaii, whatever–or it might be a very long, complex explanation, depending on what they ask. Try to avoid adding unnecessary information. If the question is, "Where was Pearl Harbor?" "Hawaii" is a sufficient response. The person doesn't need a history of the state, the exact latitude and longitude, or a description of your visit to the National Park at Pearl Harbor.

If they are asking for directions and don't have GPS reception, the answer might be quite a bit longer and more detailed. Details like "turn right at the 7-11®" might be important. If there are several gas stations on the route, or even at the same intersection, specifying which gas station could be a huge help. Directions and hours a place is open are probably the two most common kinds of questions you will experience.

Interviews

Interviews (but not interrogations) are a normal part of life. These can start as early as preschool interviews for acceptance into a competitive school and continue all the way through interviews for acceptance into a nursing home in old age. Yes, nursing homes actually do interviews because they need to be very clear on the level of care new patients need.

Do Your Research

No matter what the interview is, prepare for it in advance. Research is an important part of that preparation. If you are interviewing with a school, you should know more than just the basics of what they are best at, where they are, and the school mascot. You should know what subjects you want to study there and why you would rather study there than anywhere else with the same classes. Know the names and specialties (e.g., Early Anglo-Saxon Imagery in Poetry, not "English") for some of the instructors in the area you want to study. Learn about successful alumni and new projects the school is working on. Show them you really care and have taken the time to learn about their school, you didn't just hit send on CommonApp because it's easy and you needed a back-up school.

Later, when you are applying for a job that's more competitive than a minimum wage mall job, use those same skills. Don't show up for a job interview knowing nothing more than the first page of the corporate website tells you. Take the time to really learn what the company does, who the important execs both in the company and in the department you are applying for are. Taking an hour or an afternoon to learn more about a company, a person, or a school could make the difference between an outstanding interview that blows them out of the water (a good outcome), and you being the one blown out of the water (a bad outcome).

Dress the Part

This doesn't necessarily mean wearing a business suit. It could mean a uniform, team shirt, or a nice casual outfit. Take the time in advance to ask around (parents, teachers, counselors) to find out how you should dress. The day before the interview, decide on your outfit and make certain it is clean and presentable. If you do need to wear a suit, make certain the suit and the shirt/blouse you are wearing with it are clean and ironed.

Don't forget your shoes! While you are still growing, it sometimes happens that you realize a pair of shoes you need (cleats or dress shoes) are too small to wear and you end up wearing whatever fits. While the interviewer will undoubtedly understand, it's better to be wearing the right shoes, so take the time to check in advance and to make sure they are clean with decent (not gnarled, twisted, and stringy) laces. If your best shoes are a bit loose, you can stuff tissue paper in the toes to make them fit well enough for a short time. This isn't a good option for a longer period, like a whole day or all of prom, because it can lead to blisters, rubbed spots, and other discomfort.

Finally, while it's perfectly normal to wear white socks with sneakers, in an interview, take the time to match your socks to your pants, at least more or less. Ask an adult to confirm you are wearing the correct color. (Black is almost always a safe choice for dress socks.)

Competition/Judges Interviews

A lot of school and extracurricular activities include interviews or questioning by judges. This is a great skill to hone to help later, with job interviews. You should know the material they will be asking about extremely well because you've been working on it for months or even years. Your teachers and coaches can give you tips and pointers to give a better presentation. Listen to what they tell you because they want you to do well. It makes them look good. They will know if the judges prefer to have one person speak for the group or everyone participate when a team is being judged. They will also know if there is something specific they are looking for.

Most of the time, it's okay to talk to the judges after an event is over to see what you can do better next time. Like teachers and coaches, they are normally happy to help you improve. Sometimes they are in a hurry to leave, though, so be sure to pay attention to whether they are trying to leave or are happy to stay and chat with you.

School Interviews (including College)

An interview is a kind conversation. The interviewer is asking questions of the interviewee for some specific purpose. For school interviews, the normal purpose is twofold: ensure that you can handle the social and academic demands, and ensure that you are a good fit for their student body. The meaning of "a good fit for their student body" changes with the year and the school. Some may want all their students to be similar in interests, skills, and outlook, while others seek variety. This is something that is usually not too hard to find out and will help you know, in advance, if you are likely to be a good fit. If you have done a good job of researching the school, you probably have a good idea of what they are looking for and what about you is likely to appeal most to them.

No matter how much you prepare, there are always things beyond your control. Some years they might already have a great orchestra, sports teams, and other activities, while other years they might need students to play certain instruments, play a certain position on a team, or fill another empty slot. There is no way to know in advance. Sometimes you "fail" an interview for reasons totally beyond your control (they really needed a bass player/hockey goalie), and sometimes you "pass" for reasons you never would have guessed were important (you are a bass player/hockey goalie).

Job Interviews

When you are old enough to work, the first step in getting a job is filling out an application. The second is having an interview. As you move up in your career, you will be interviewed many more times for many more jobs. When you are looking at a higher-level job, there may easily be four or five rounds of interviews, starting with a recruiter and ending with a half day to a day of interviews with multiple people. Because it isn't something that happens every day, most people aren't very comfortable being interviewed.

Interrogations

Most of the time, people asking you questions don't think you've done anything wrong, but an interrogation is different. When you are being interrogated, the person interrogating you thinks you have done something wrong, like committing a crime or spying. In a true interrogation, the interrogator is a law enforcement officer (police officer, intelligence agent, etc.) and you have certain rights that must not be violated, although those rights vary wildly depending on where you are. In the Stalin-era USSR, they were…limited.

Most questions, including most interviews, are asked in either a friendly or neutral way. Interrogations are not friendly, or even neutral. The questioning tends to be forceful and intimidating because they are trying to get you to admit wrongdoing or criminal activity. No one expects average people to withstand actual interrogation. Navy Seals, Army Rangers, Special Ops, spies, and other people in highly specialized fields with knowledge of national security managers are trained in resisting interrogation and even then, they can't always resist.

It is highly unlikely you will ever be in a true interrogation. If you are, it will probably be by local police investigating a local crime, not some kind of secret police or national intelligence agency. American police are required to read you something called your "Miranda Rights" which include the right to an attorney. If you can't pay for one, the government will. Tell them "I want my attorney, I do not wish to speak with you until I have contact with my attorney." You also need to call your family to let them know where you are as soon as possible.

Activity

Find someone to do a mock job interview where you are the one trying to get a job, or go on an actual job interview.

Quick Quiz

T/F   Interrogations are a common part of everyday life in the US.

T/F   No one has interviews before they are adults going on job interviews.

T/F   Interviews, interrogations, and questioning are all the same.

T/F   It is a good idea to practice before you have a job interview.

T/F   No matter what the subject, research it before any interview.

Resources

Articles

Difference Between Interview and Interrogation
www.differencebetween.com/difference-between-interview-and-vs-interrogation/

Interviewing, Questioning, and Interrogation
pressbooks.bccampus.ca/criminalinvestigation/chapter/chapter-9-interviewing-questioning-and-interrogation/

Miranda Rights
www.mirandarights.org/

Your Right to Privacy
www.aclu.org/your-right-privacy

Books

Conversational Camouflage: Oratory Discretion and Pretexting for Behavioral Concealment by Matthew Dermody

Crucial Conversations: Tools for Talking When Stakes are High by Kerry Patterson, Joseph Grenny, Ron McMillan, and Al Switzler

The Soft Answer: Verbal T'ai Chi for Sociable Self Defense by Susan Lowell de Solorzano, Kathryn Lydon, Monica Schoettler, and Rita Solorzano

Videos

6 MOST Difficult Interview Questions and How to Answer Them
www.youtube.com/watch?v=bQ1DovMfgxw

Answering Tough Questions [business focused]
www.youtube.com/watch?v=hSeAGSPDG4w

Dealing with Intrusive People Part 1 and Part 2
www.youtube.com/watch?v=eS6hgauTuS4/

Former FBI Agent Explains How to Read Body Language |

Tradecraft | WIRED
www.youtube.com/watch?v=4jwUXV4QaTw

Get That Job – Interviews, a Conversation Not An Interrogation
www.youtube.com/watch?v=aL8d6ayabpo

How to Gracefully Answer Nosy Questions
www.youtube.com/watch?v=zpja12vLvk8

How Not to Interview: WorkAustin.com
www.youtube.com/watch?v=GvU8fL4MiSQ

It's None of Their Business: How to Stop Over-explaining Yourself to Nosy, Intrusive People
www.youtube.com/watch?v=VNnKr2AGGh4

The Lie Guy Channel: Interviewing and Interrogation Techniques
www.youtube.com/user/TheLieGuy

Succeeding at the College Admissions Interview
www.youtube.com/watch?v=4qY9icExjEw

{PART 6}
SELF DEFENSE

First and foremost, **a successful fight is one you walk away from**. If you can do that without having physically engaged, it is definitely a win. With that said, if you can't defend yourself, you may not survive long in a disaster. In daily life, few of us really have to defend ourselves, but disasters are a very different matter. And there are times, and places, where self-defense is very important. The smaller you are, physically, the more important it is because you look like an easier victim. **When you look like an easy victim, predators will try to prey on you.** That's just how it nature works.

I am not a lawyer or law enforcement officer. I cannot speak to legal consequences of self-defense.

Self-defense is about surviving. Do not instigate trouble. Walk away, unless you or someone else is in imminent danger. If it's someone else, do you care enough to risk your life for them? Do not let pride or arrogance trap you into making a fatal mistake. That includes turning your back on someone intent on hurting you as surely as it includes escalating a fight when you could have safely walked away.

It is important to really understand what a life or death situation is: There is a very real chance someone will die. This is not figurative or exaggerated. If you are in a life or death situation, you may be forced to kill the other person in self-defense. If you are not able to do that, it may result in you dying. If there is no real chance of you dying, it's not life-or-death. If you are not prepared to badly injure or even kill the other person, you may hesitate at a critical moment and die.

That is life or death. Hurt feelings, injured pride, bullying, none of these are life or death or even physically threatening (with the possible exception of bullying).

Killing another person is, and should be, extraordinarily difficult for neuro-typical people. When it comes down to it, even those who have extensive military training and experience sometimes hesitate to take a killing blow. That is simply the cold hard reality. If you think you can kill another, know that the odds are that you are wrong. Be prepared for that as well.

Killing isn't always necessary, even in a life-or-death situation. Incapacitating is almost always sufficient. Sometimes your attacker will simply run off after being injured, even if they meant to kill you. Accept that and stop when you and yours are safe. <u>Take the time to read the article "Being a Knife Fighter" listed in Resources for this chapter. It does an outstanding job of explaining the importance of de-escalation for your own sake.</u>

Unarmed Self Defense: The easiest way to never be truly unarmed and unable to defend yourself is to have your body be your weapon.

Simple Weapons: Sticks, slingshots, bats, even thrown dirt are among the simplest weapons. Most can be improvised from found items if you are out and find yourself in a dangerous situation.

Guns and Gun Safety: Not everyone either likes or wants firearms, and that's okay. What is important is to learn how to handle a firearm safely, *even if there isn't one in your home.* Guns cannot, and do not, shoot themselves. Regardless of whether you own firearms yourself, if you do not know how to handle one, you could accidentally shoot yourself or someone else. While it's easy to sit in your home and declare that you would never touch a firearm and no one can make you, it's much harder (and potentially foolish) to stick to that if you are caught in an alley and have the chance to grab a criminal's firearm and run to safety.

{TWENTY-FOUR}

UNARMED SELF-DEFENSE

There are times people have to use weapons to defend themselves. There are other times people cannot use weapons to defend themselves. They may not have weapons, or weapons might do too much damage, including accidentally hitting bystanders or people behind the target. That's when unarmed self-defense is useful.

"Unarmed self-defense" automatically brings to mind ninjas and martial arts of all sorts, but that is definitely not the only form of unarmed self-defense. **Skunks have what may be one of the most effective unarmed self-defense systems on the planet.** There is no creature that has been subjected to their stench that will deliberately injure, or even frighten, a skunk. Despite being incredibly slow with virtually no other defenses, skunks are safe.

If you realize you are in a dangerous situation, it is important to think beyond what you see in movies and on TV. Those things are not real. They are choreographed *at least* as carefully as the most elaborate ballet, and they have massive safeguards to prevent injuries. In real life, injuries are real and there are no crash pads or medics on stand-by if things go wrong.

Remember the skunk. Think beyond just injuring the threat. Avoiding seeming like a target in the first place and, if spotted, looking like too much work for the return are far more likely to keep you safe than any weapon or active self-defense on the planet. Don't believe it? Ask any law enforcement officer.

The Environment

The words "the environment" generally brings up images of nature, but the larger definition of it is everything around you. For example, your home environment includes a kitchen, TV, bedrooms, parents, siblings, pets, stuffed animals, a yard, and everything else around you. In self-defense, using your environment could mean throwing a blanket from the sofa over an attacker's head or sand/dirt/table salt at their eyes so they can't see while you (try to) escape. It could mean using garden tools or a broom to help keep them too far away to grab you. It could even mean using your knowledge of what is around to find a good place to hide until you can escape safely.

The environment also includes the people around you and their emotions. This was discussed more in the section on using your words, but the emotions of the people around you can impact your safety. Don't ignore them. As discussed, your words can also impact your environment. If you can use your words to defuse a situation before it ever gets to any physical form of self-defense, that's a win.

Martial Arts

There are tons of different martial arts and each one is slightly different. In terms of self-defense, they range from Tai Chai, a popular Chinese form that focuses on slow controlled moves, to Krav Maga, an unarmed self-defense technique developed for the Israeli National Defense Force. Picking a martial art is, or should be, about more than just finding the closest one or the one your friend goes to. Making a list of studios near you that your family can afford is a good first step, but it is only the first step. The heart of the matter will be deciding which martial art and which instructor best suit you as the student.

Studio reputation matters, to a degree. Some people will think well of a studio based on what awards the instructors and students have earned. If you want to go into competition, that may really matter to you, but for learning self-defense, it really doesn't. A kick to the gut with less-than-perfect form is still a kick to the gut and will still leave the bad guy doubled over, if it's powerful enough.

If you haven't watched *Karate Kid*, you should. The "bad guy" dojo has a good reputation because of how many competitions they have won while Mr. Miyagi has no reputation because he doesn't run a dojo. And yet, of course Mr. Miyagi is the better teacher. Don't ignore reputation, but remember that it isn't the most important aspect when you make your choice. Listening to/reading what others say about it will give you a good idea about how they really teach. Advertising materials do give you some clues, if you look at them carefully. If they *say* they focus on kids, but their brochures do not *show* a single child in class, the odds are they aren't really child-focused, for example. Studios can be strict, nurturing, youth-focused, adult-focused, etc. and each has its place. "Strict" may sound bad and "nurturing" may sound good, but it isn't that simple. One person's "nurturing" is another person's "unstructured," and that makes learning difficult or even impossible. "Strict" can also mean "structured", which can make learning a lot easier.

Since there is a lot of personal preference and personality that goes into choosing studio, after you narrow down your choices, take the time to visit the dojo and observe it. Watching the actual instructor teaching and taking a free sample class really is the best way to evaluate if the dojo is the right fit. Instruction quality and how well the teaching style suits you personally, as the student, are far more important than any awards the studio or instructor may have. An instructor with a lot of awards, and even with a lot of students who think she is great, may simply be a poor personality fit for you.

If you, as a student, truly aren't comfortable with a teacher after a few introductory classes, talk to your parents. It may not be the right dojo for you, or it may not be the right martial art. There is nothing wrong with changing dojos, although your parents will almost certainly expect you to stay for a while after they fork over money for studio-specific gear so make sure to let them know sooner rather than later if you are uncomfortable.

Wrestling

This isn't the first thing that comes to mind for most people, but if you know wrestling, the skill could help you stay safe if someone attacks you. One of the most basic things it can help you with is knocking an opponent to the ground, especially if they don't know wrestling moves themselves. By itself, wrestling isn't going to keep you safe, but it is a good skill in combination with other physical skills, such as martial arts.

Words

Words don't always work, but they can be used to decrease the danger in some situations. Don't dismiss "using your words" just because it's something you start hearing in preschool. Wouldn't you rather be able to just walk away from a bad situation without you or the ones you care about being injured?

Words are most effective in either a one on one situation or when one person is able to directly address a large group. If they can't hear your words, they won't help. In a large scale event like a riot, they won't keep you truly safe, but the right words in the right tone might help you deflect individuals looking to attack you, giving you more time to escape to safety.

Apologize

In many situations, the single most effective way to deflect fighting and danger using your words may be to simply apologize, and apologize well. And yes, you can apologize badly. When you apologize, address the person directly. Admit what you did wrong, say you are sorry, and don't make excuses or insult the person to whom you are apologizing. And don't bring in any outside events that may have occurred, including things that happened in the past or with other people. That rarely helps.

An apology really doesn't cost anything. It can cost you emotionally, but only if you let it. If you have difficulty apologizing, try viewing it as a way to make the other person or people feel better, like a verbal salve on an emotional injury. That's really what it is. Take a minute to apply it. Even if you have not done anything wrong, an apology may still help. Misperceptions and misunderstandings have led to a lot of violence throughout human history. The person who is angry with you may truly believe you did something wrong. A simple apology is a good way to help them calm down.

Finally, yes, this was covered in an earlier chapter, but apologizing can be hard and it's an important skill to at least be comfortable with.

Tone

The tone of your voice makes a massive difference in whether your words help to calm a situation, or make it worse. Imagine your parents tell you to apologize to your sibling. You have a choice between saying "so-o-o-rrreee" (making it three to four syllables instead of two) or "I'm sorry for deleting your progress on that game. It was an accident and I won't do it again." Will both have the same effect or will one lead to your parents (and sibling) yelling more?

Think about your friends and family. When something goes wrong and they yell at you or use an angry voice, does that make it better or worse? For most people, they find themselves becoming more angry when the people around them use angry or judgmental voice and calmer when they use a quieter, calmer voice. It's a physiological reaction we cannot easily control.

There is also a chance you will find yourself in a situation with a bully or other dangerous person who views "calm" as "weak" and, in that very rare situation, being belligerent and angry might seem to serve you better. However, that situation is extremely rare and even then, a firm, confident tone is a safer choice than angry and belligerent. A calm tone is far more likely to help you salvage a bad situation and stay safe.

Volume

Volume matters too. You can be very, very angry and very, very quiet but most people associate loud with angry, not quiet. There is a reason "don't raise your voice with me!" is a parental refrain that probably goes back to the Neanderthals. Loud voices automatically seem more ready to fight than quiet voices. On top of that, being loud draws attention. If you need to escape a dangerous area, attention is the last thing you want. While there is nothing wrong with being loud in and of itself, being aware of when and where that is (and is not) appropriate is just plain smart.

One time, I spoke in front of our local county elected officials because I was most displeased with what they were doing. I did not raise my voice beyond my normal speaking range. I did not gesture angrily. I simply spoke, but my tone made it crystal-clear that I was very angry with them. The people who heard me speak said I yelled at them. But I didn't do it with volume. I did it with tone. The only time you need to be loud is if the other person literally cannot hear you otherwise.

Activity

Look around where you are right now. Talk about what you could use to defend yourself and how you could use it.

Quick Quiz

T/F   A blanket, pillow, or other nearby objects can be used in unarmed combat.

T/F   Sand and dirt are never used in unarmed combat.

T/F   Earning a black belt is an impressive accomplishment.

T/F   "Using your words" with someone who is angry is stupid.

T/F   An apology has never stopped a fight.

Resources

Articles

5 Best Improvised Weapons in the World
lowtechcombat.com/blog/2012/01/5-best-improvised-weapons-in-world

*Dealing with Angry People
www.mindtools.com/pages/article/dealing-with-angry-people.htm

*How to Choose the Best Martial Arts School for Your Child
www.selfgrowth.com/articles/How_To_Choose_The_Best_Martial_Arts_School_
For_Your_Child.html

How to Deal with Verbal Confrontation
streetfightsecrets.wordpress.com/2010/09/09/how-to-deal-with-verbal-confrontation/

The Five Ingredients of An Effective Apology
www.psychologytoday.com/us/blog/the-squeaky-wheel/201311/the-five-
ingredients-effective-apology

Hand-to-Hand: 8 Best Martial Arts for Self Defense
hiconsumption.com/best-martial-arts-for-self-defense/

How to Apologize More Sincerely
www.verywellmind.com/how-to-apologize-more-sincerely-3144467

*How to Apologize Sincerely & Effectively
www.perfectapology.com/how-to-apologize.html

Improvised Self Defense Weapons: How to Turn Everyday Objects

to Your Advantage
blackbeltmag.com/techniques/self-defense/improvised-self-defense-weapons-how-to-turn-everyday-objects-to-your-advantage

Improvised Weapons Found in the Street
selfdefensetutorials.com/improvised-weapons-found-in-the-street/

Improvised Weapons: Self-Defense in the Real World
offgridsurvival.com/improvisedweapons-selfdefense/

Is Wrestling Good for Self Defense?
www.sportzbits.com/blog/is-wrestling-good-for-self-defense/

Your Tone of Voice Affects How People Respond to You
www.impactcommunicationsinc.com/pdf/nwsltr_2001/ICINwsltrph0106.pdf

Books

Complete Beginner's Guide to Picking a Martial Art by Chad Kunego

*A Cup of Coffee: And Other Improvised Weapons of Self Defense by Pat Smith

Facing Violence: Preparing for the Unexpected by Rory Miller

A Guide to Improvised Weaponry: How to Protect Yourself with Whatever You've Got by Terry Schappert and Adam Slutsky

How to Street Fight: Street Fighting Techniques for Learning Self Defense by Sam Fury and Shumona Mallick

Street Survival Guide: Self Defense Awareness, Avoidance and Fighting Techniques by Rory Christensen

Survive the Unthinkable: A Total Guide to Women's Self-Protection by Tim Larkin

When Violence is the Answer: Learning How to Do What it Takes When Your Life is at Stake by Tim Larkin

Violence of Mind: Training and Preparation for Extreme Violence by Varg Freeborn

Videos

7 Mistakes to Avoid When Choosing A Martial Arts School in Keller (one is how well they clean the dojo)
www.youtube.com/watch?v=sHRRMWb9VVU

How to Apologize
www.youtube.com/watch?v=z3H_GgtE3Tc

How to Use a Belt as an Improvised Weapon
www.youtube.com/watch?v=QfU8BxiZ9Os

Improvised Self Defense Items for WROL
www.youtube.com/watch?v=w1db89I6IT8

Line of Takedown Defense: Basic Wrestling Moves and Techniques for Beginners
www.youtube.com/watch?v=h1vlqBRmH_g

Martial Arts Tips: How to Choose a Martial Art to Learn
www.youtube.com/watch?v=osLdP29jefw

*What to Do When Someone Doesn't Accept Your Apology
www.youtube.com/watch?v=7oh3yGV9B50

Wrestling as Self Defense
www.youtube.com/watch?v=MiZU44j0_pA

{TWENTY-FIVE}

SIMPLE WEAPONS

Throughout history, humans have used all kinds of weapons, some of which are clearly, and solely, weapons. Swords, throwing stars, light sabers, and bows are just a few of the many hand-held weapons warriors have used throughout the ages. It may seem like these have nothing in common but there is one huge commonality: It takes a moment to pick them up, but a lifetime to master.

Some simple weapons, such as bats, knives, and poles, can be used without any training but even with those, practice makes them more effective. For most weapons, including those, even small amounts of practice will dramatically increase your effectiveness. Truly mastering any weapon generally requires hundreds or even thousands of hours of drilling and practicing. Very few people outside of the military spend that much time with any weapon, for good reason. For basic self-defense, that level of skill simply isn't necessary. Think of the scene with Indiana Jones in the marketplace. He was fighting a master swordsmen and was, himself, pretty much a master of his bullwhip. And yet, he won that fight by pulling a firearm and shooting the master swordsmen from a distance. Having the right tool for the situation is critical.

In fact, most of us don't carry any weapon regularly and even if we do, it might not be easily accessible when needed. Today, there are also a lot of places where you aren't allowed to carry weapons and they back that up with metal detectors to ensure no one is carrying. That's why unarmed self-defense is always a great skill to have, but as Indy shows us, sometimes weapons are needed. Unlike firearms, some, but not all, simple weapons can be improvised from readily available the materials. (True improvised weapons were discussed in the chapter on unarmed self-defense.) Others, such as a bow and arrows, require training, special equipment, and the correct materials. Quality swords, throwing stars, and knives require even more skill, materials, and equipment.

Bow and Arrows

Bow and arrows developed all over the world, so there are more than a few kinds of them, but the three most common are variations on the long bow, cross bow, and compound bow. It is even theoretically possible to make one yourself in the woods, but don't expect it to be easy or effective. Making a functional, much less good, bow and good arrows requires skill and a great deal of practice. Unless you have those, simply buy one and make sure to always retrieve your arrows after you shoot them, unless doing so would endanger you.

With the proper tools and equipment, you can learn to make your own arrows. Kids do it at Scout camp. However, it's easiest to buy them. They are available anywhere from Walmart® to high-end sporting goods stores and specialty retailers.

When you decide to buy one, find a good store and have them fit you for both the bow and the arrows. The bow needs to fit your body, including a draw weight that you can manage, and the arrows need to fit your draw length. A half dozen arrows will give you a good start. In addition, buy a shooting glove, bow wax, and possibly a quiver and a case, especially for a compound bow. More specialized stores have the staff to help ensure the arrows fit you too. Fit is more important with archery equipment than with some other weaponry.

Recurve and long bows should be stored unstrung, but compound bows are kept strung. It is important that bows be stored away from high humidity, which can warp the wood, and extreme heat/cold, which can also damage the wood, and that you take the time to learn proper care for both the bow and the arrows.

Clubs and Bats

War clubs are rare outside of video games. They require enormous brute strength to do real damage because they weigh a lot. While it is possible to injure someone badly by hitting a vulnerable spot hard enough, using a club brings you close enough to your opponent to risk being grabbed by them, and war clubs really do require enormous strength. While simple to use and to improvise, a club should definitely not be your first choice for defense. Its best use is probably to slow down your opponent enough to allow you to escape, get help, or reach a better weapon.

A bat is smaller, lighter, easier to swing, and easier to find, and they come in a variety of materials including aluminum and wood. Like a war club, a bat brings combatants far too close for comfort, but unlike a club, bats aren't particularly heavy and most people have used them at least a few times as a kid. Even small people can comfortably wield a bat. Because bats are small and light, it is easy to put more force into the actual swing and to do real damage. The smaller size also makes it easier to break a bat than many other weapons, rendering it useless.

Knives

Probably the only weapon that comes to mind before a knife in the modern world is a gun. Knives are easy to find, easy to carry, easy to use, and have been around nearly as long as mankind. The two most obvious dangers of a knife fight are being within arms-reach of your opponent and being injured by your own knife. **The simple truth is that knife fights are extremely dangerous and best avoided,** if at all possible. Do not *ever* threaten another person with a knife, and be very careful how badly you injure another in self-defense. There is a video by Tim Kennedy in the Resources section of this chapter that does a good job of explaining how bad knife fights can be.

There is a high probability the police will become involved with a knife fight, just like they would with a gun fight. Unlike a gun that can have the ammo removed or spent, a knife blade is always there. Compared to a gun, people have a great deal more control over how badly they injure another with a knife. Once a bullet leaves a firearm, it pretty much continues on its trajectory until the momentum is spent. Sometimes, the brass from a bullet can be "reloaded" and used again after it is fired, but that takes time, tools, knowledge, and supplies. A bullet can't just be reused. Once a knife has cut a person, it can immediately be removed, pushed in deeper, moved around to create ever greater damage, etc.

While it is easy to find "a" knife, some knives are more dangerous in a knife fight than others. If you face an attacker armed with a knife, there is a good chance they have a knife that is more dangerous in a knife-fight than anything you might grab in the kitchen, and experience that makes them more dangerous in a knife fight. (Remember how this chapter started with the importance of practice?) Or they could be someone high on drugs who literally can't feel much pain, has no training, and will just keep coming at you long past when they would have dropped if they weren't on drugs.

If you are in a position where a knife fight is your best chance for survival, do your best to keep moving to stay out of your opponents range. Moving in and out to injure your opponent without being injured yourself is part of a knife fight, but it is almost inevitable that you will be cut in a knife fight. Being mentally prepared to see your own blood flowing, dripping, etc., should help you remain focused on the key tasks of self-defense: disarming your opponent and staying safe. Once the assailant is disarmed and it is safe to leave, do so, keeping in mind legal requirements to contact law enforcement and notify them of what has happened.

Martial Arts Weapons

Throwing stars, nunchakus, tonfa. Many different kinds of weapons are used in the martial arts. They tend to be small and/or easily improvised, but higher-quality ones perform better. Don't dismiss them as mere toys or distractions from "real" fighting techniques just because of their simplicity. With such a variety of tools, discussing them is beyond the scope of this book, but martial arts weapons are definitely worth learning.

Poles/Staffs

If you are facing someone wielding a knife, it's better to stay out of slashing range. What's the best way to do that? De-escalate and walk away, but the next best is the use the simplest of all weapons, a pole or stick. This is one weapon that can be improvised easily and used to block attacks. In martial arts, one common type is a Bo staff.

Light staffs are easier for beginners but cause less damage than heavier staffs. As mentioned with clubs and bats, the lighter weight makes it easier for smaller people to carry, easier to put more force into the swing (as opposed to relying on the weight of the weapon to do the damage), and easier to break. No matter what the size, poles and staffs are not easily concealed, although they are fairly easy to camouflage, especially if they are more the size of a can than of something Gandalf would carry. People may see them, but they don't have to realize they are a weapon.

As with other weapons, learning how to use a Bo staff is beyond the scope of this book. It isn't for everyone, but if you like to use a walking stick anyway, this might be a great choice for you to learn.

SIMPLE WEAPONS

Slingshots

David slew Goliath with a slingshot. You are not David, but a slingshot is still a very simple weapon to use and to make. Like most weapons, it takes a great deal of practice to become well and truly good with a sling-shot, and without practice, it is all too easy to get badly injured by treating it as a toy. Slingshots are inexpensive to buy. The best ammo is as solid and round as possible, although random rocks and other items can be used in a pinch. It needs to be centered in the pouch to help with aiming. Hold the base with your dominant hand and pull back your ammo with the other one. When the band is aimed and completely stretched, release the shot. Alternately, if there is no way to get a stretchy band, the user may swing the sling until it is fast enough, then release the ammo.

Other

There are lots of other unusual, rarely seen weapons like maces and two-handed swords. They look really cool, but are large and unwieldy. These aren't easy to carry around with you or conceal in your home, although it is certainly possible to hang them on a wall as decorations, leaving them within easy reach.

Maintenance

It doesn't matter whether you are talking about a good pair of boots, a car engine, or a simple staff: Equipment needs to be taken care of, including cleaning and repair. Remove any dirt, blood, rust, or other potentially-damaging buildup every single time you use them, *before putting it away*. Make sure to wipe items dry. Be sure they are fully dry before putting them away to prevent mold, mildew, rust, decay, and other water damage.

Many items, including both wood and metal, need to be oiled periodically to remain in good condition. Different kinds of wood and metal need different oils, so you will need to research what is best for your particular items.

Activity

Make or buy one or more of the weapons from this section and practice with it.

Quick Quiz

T/F   Humidity is good for weapons. Try to store them in the most humid spot in your house.

T/F   Poles/staffs are arguably the simplest weapons.

T/F   "Simple" weapons may take many years to truly master.

T/F   Maintain a blood circle when using a knife or bladed weapon.

T/F   War clubs are common in modern America.

Resources

Articles

*Being a Knife Fighter
www.nononsenseselfdefense.com/knifefighter.html

Complete Beginner's Guide to Bo Staff
www.blackbeltathome.com/the-complete-beginners-guide-to-bo-staff/

How I Make Arrows
poorfolkbows.com/arrow1.htm

How to Make a Bow and Arrow By Hand
www.popularmechanics.com/home/how-to-plans/how-to/a17108/make-a-bow-and-arrow-by-hand/

How to Make a Slingshot
www.wikihow.com/Make-a-Sling-Shot

Knife Fighting Techniques
www.sammyfranco.com/knife-fighting-techniques.html

Other

Slinging
www.slinging.org/

Scouting-Specific

Archery Merit Badge
meritbadge.org/wiki/index.php/Archery

Videos

Bo Staff Spinning Tutorial for Beginners
www.youtube.com/watch?v=gm5D8TS3mNY

How to Make a Homemade Target Arrow With Feathers and a Hand
Forged Arrowhead
www.youtube.com/watch?v=6-CRPtTTRWI

How to Make Primitive Arrows
www.youtube.com/watch?v=iNWesh15MrM

How to Use a Sling Underarm Style Ancient Sling
www.instructables.com/id/HOW-to-use-a-SLING-Underarm-style-Ancient-Sling/

Indiana Jones – Knife to a Gun Fight
www.youtube.com/watch?v=ua_TZ84hmEA

*Tim Kennedy discusses knife fighting at SHOT Show 2016
www.youtube.com/watch?v=hxw7eazSJjk

{TWENTY-SIX}

GUNS AND GUN SAFETY

1. ALWAYS keep guns pointed in a safe direction.

2. ALWAYS keep your finger off the trigger until ready to shoot.

3. ALWAYS keep guns unloaded until ready to shoot.

4. ALWAYS treat EVERY firearm as if it is loaded.

Some people seem to fear that any exposure to any guns will cause a person to suddenly become a crazed killer and go on a rampage. In fact, exposure to firearms lowers curiosity and can ingrain solid safety habits. This makes sense if you think about it. It is human nature to be curious about that which is new and to want to try new things. Everyone has seen pictures and videos of firearms in use. This can lead to a natural interest in handling them, including putting fingers on the trigger and even starting to pull just to see what it feels like. It is all too easy for that to lead to tragedy.

> **Note:** In the military, guns are on ships and tanks. If a human being can lift it using their own strength, it's far too small to be a "gun." People who are in, or have associated with those in, the military commonly uses the term "weapon" instead of "gun."

Basic gun safety training is important because it takes care of that curiosity. When you go through gun safety training, you handle one or more firearms and may have the chance to fire one as well. Your age, local laws, available facilities, and other factors influence whether you can fire a weapon when you go through basic gun safety training or it it's just "book learning." You can receive some basic gun safety instruction in a living room, but you certainly can't fire a gun there!

As with other forms of self-defense, practice makes perfect. In this case, target practice at a range. Quite a few hunters have spent enough time with, and money on, their rifles to be highly accurate with them, but hunting rifles are simply not something anyone uses for every-day carry. It is important to practice with each weapon you might use. If you carry a handgun, practice with that one. If you have a shotgun for home defense, practice with that one. Other concerns may dictate practicing with a less expensive firearm or one that uses less expensive or easier to find ammo, but it is still important to practice and be familiar with each weapon.

Cleaning your firearm after each use is recommended to keep it in top condition but a firearm isn't like a dinner dish: you can use a dirty firearm (within limits). Storage in a gun safe is recommended but people do not always do that. Periodic repairs, replacement of parts, and thorough cleaning are all highly recommended but easy to skip over. Unlike most things today, firearms are generally built to last through hard use and generations of owners, but that isn't a guarantee. You need to clean them, keep them safe, and repair them as needed to ensure they last for your life and beyond.

If you ever have a firearm of your own, you will need to learn some more advanced safety measures (such as storage) as well as basic maintenance and cleaning. You will also need to learn about firearm and hunting laws in your state.

What to do if you find a gun

DO NOT HANDLE IT unless you need to take it from someone who is handling it in an unsafe manner. If you do need to take it, put it somewhere safe as soon as possible. A firearm simply cannot fire if the trigger isn't pulled. Find an adult, preferably the one who owns or lives in the building you are in, and have them secure it. **If there is no adult available,** leave the room or area and keep everyone else out of it until an adult returns and can secure it. If that isn't possible either, someone needs to move the firearm to a safer, less accessible location. **Under no circumstance should anyone either point a firearm at another person or put their finger on the trigger.** This is covered in more detail in the section on safety, but is important enough to be repeated frequently.

Training

If your first exposure to handling a firearm is being trained in safety, the firearm you are handling should be unloaded, safety on, and you will have just been instructed in safe handling. All of this combined leads to the worst likely injury being getting a finger pinched. If, on the other hand, your first exposure is when you find a gun someone has hidden for self-defense, it will probably be loaded, the chances of you remembering gun safety rules are slim to none (if you ever even heard them), and there is a very high chance of someone being hurt, even killed.

Get real life, in-person training where you handle real, honest-to-god firearms and possibly even shoot them, if appropriate. It's the most important thing you can do to remain safe around firearms.

Safety

If a gun is pointed at something, that means the shooter intends, or is at least considering, to shoot it. If you have a gun pointed at your sibling, that means you are literally willing to shoot them, which will result in jail time and a ruined future for you. **Do not point a firearm at another human being unless it is a genuine life-or-death situation.** That means there is a Bad Guy in the room who will kill someone else or cripple them for life if they are not stopped.

Ear and Eye Pro

Protecting your eyes and ears is important no matter what you are doing, but even more so when you are firing a gun because they are loud and things are flying around, primarily casings. There can also be smoke, especially with black powder firearms. The latter type are primarily historical and not a lot of people use them, but they are sometimes used, especially by re-enactors.

Firing a gun is noisy. Some more so than others, but even with a noise suppressor (a "silencer"), it's not silent. The more often you are around shooting, the more important ear protection (ear pro) becomes. Noise over 140 decibels can cause hearing damage and most firearms produce *at least* 140 decibels of noise, some substantially more depending on caliber and conditions. Being in an enclosed space such as an indoor range or a hunting blind can cause the sound to reverberate and do significantly <u>more</u> damage.

This makes ear pro non-optional. The cheapest ear pro is also considered to be arguably the best, and incredibly easy to carry with you at all times: those little moldable orange ear plugs that come a hundred or so in a plastic pail. These can be used with more expensive electronic earmuff style headphones that block out any loud noises. The earmuffs make it easier to have a conversation on the range because they only block loud sounds, like gunfire or yelling. Normal conversation isn't affected.

Basic eye protection (eye pro) is important too. We've all seen guns fired on TV, if nowhere else. The empty casing being ejected is clearly visible on the shows, and it happens with most firearms in real life. (Revolvers are one exception.) Imagine one of those hitting your eye at speed and you will understand why eye pro is so important. Eye pro can be as simple as a cheap pair of sunglasses, but those have obvious drawbacks when you are shooting inside or in low light situations. For that reason, most people buy shooting glasses, which can be quite inexpensive. If you have particularly strong prescription glasses and shoot often, it may be worth the expense to buy custom prescription shooting glasses, but very few people need these. The regular cheap glasses are easy enough to fit over regular glasses.

Eye pro and ear pro are not terms I created. They are commonly used on ranges and by anyone using firearms, such as hunters. Learn and use both the terms and the items they refer to.

When you finish shooting, and before you eat anything, wash your hands to remove lead residue.

Range Safety

Check the basic range safety rules for any range you use. The basic rules are quite standard, but the details vary. It is common to not permit holstered weapon on the range at all, but clearly anyone who carries on a regular basis needs to practice drawing their firearm and shooting. Therefore, some ranges allow drawing and shooting under certain specific circumstances.

First and foremost, cease fire means exactly that: cease fire. It does not mean after one more shot, or think about stopping soon. If someone says cease fire, stop shooting immediately. Remove your finger from the trigger (if it's there), put your firearm down, and take a step back. To make this very clear: after cease fire is called, you should not be touching your firearm at all. It should be perfectly safe for someone to walk downrange in front of your firearm.

If you cannot manage following this rule, get off the range. Immediately. Do not return until you can.

Calling ceasefire will result in the range going from hot to cold immediately. In this context, hot and cold mean the same as they do in hot war and cold war, although a hot war is really only called a war since most are hot. "Hot" means guns are being fired and you are at risk of being shot if you are on the range. On a cold range, firearms are not being handled. No shots will be fired downrange until it is once again hot, so it safe to walk on the range.

Normally, anyone can call ceasefire when and if they see a dangerous situation but the range officer (the person in charge) will be the one to call a cease fire to allow everyone to clean up their area, police (pick up) their brass, and change their targets. You should never call cease fire without a reason, but you should always call ceasefire if the range is hot and a person or animal wanders onto the range. Ranges normally go cold following a schedule of either time or events. This means a range could be scheduled to be cold from 25 to 30 after the hour and every half hour thereafter, or it could be after a set group of shooters fire a certain number of times.

The firing line is a line beyond which no one may pass on a hot range. Anything downrange may be shot but each person generally knows what they can and should be firing at. Each shooter who is on the firing line has their own place to stand. This normally includes some sort of table to hold their gun, ammo, magazines, and any other personal items.

> **Note:** A clip goes inside a magazine, which is then inserted into a semi-automatic firearm. The words "clip" and "magazine" denote different items and are not interchangeable.

Hunter Safety

First and foremost, **take a state-sponsored hunter safety course**.

Second, don't go out alone. Accidents happen, even to those with a lot of experience. Something as simple as sliding down a hill can become life-threatening. How? By getting a leg or foot impaled on a branch and needing to travel back to your vehicle or cabin for help, especially if the weather or cell service is bad. It happens more often than you would think.

It's hardly a secret: hunters wear **safety orange** (a.k.a., blaze orange, hunter orange, OSHA orange). It may not always be the law, but it's always a good idea. There are two primary groups whose appearance is designed to blend into their surroundings: the military and prey animals. Predators have less need to blend in because they aren't trying to hide from anything else. Don't look like prey. Wear safety orange and be clearly visible as a hunter, not prey.

Tree stands are popular because they make it easy to see a long distance and harder for prey to detect hunters, but they are also a leading cause of hunter injuries. Sitting up in a tree, motionless, for a long time makes it all too easy to fall asleep, and fall out of the tree stand. Using a full-body harness is the best way to stay safe in a tree stand. Owning a harness does nothing to keep you safe unless you actually use it, and a harness that isn't designed for someone who weighs as much as you weigh with all your gear included may not do you much good either.

- Watch the short online course "Tree Stand Safety" in the Resources section of this chapter.

- Read the instructions for your tree stand and practice setting it up using a tree of approximately the right size before you go hunting.

- Your gun should be *unloaded* when you use a haul line to pull it up to or down from your tree stand, to reduce the chance of an accident.

- Harness yourself in as soon as possible. One man I know fell and broke his neck while he was in the process of securing his harness to the tree.

- Inspect your tree stand, including chains and straps, regularly for wear and damage, including rust and missing bolts.

Hunting blinds are small shelters with spaces hunters look and shoot through. They are popular because hunters can sit inside, out of the weather and harder for prey to see or smell. One downside is that shots can reverberate and seem louder inside the box, so shooting high caliber weapons even with ear pro is not advised. Another is that people like to use heaters to stay warm and cozy in cold weather and blinds are often made of flammable materials. It's important to use a heater that has a tip-over safety shut-off valve and a low-oxygen shut-off to remain safe, if you feel you must use a heater in a blind.

Cleaning

Cleaning and maintenance are as important for a gun as they are for anything else. Like most things, you can be compulsive and take the time to ensure every last speck of dust and grit is cleaned off every time you fire even a single shot, but the reality is that is time consuming and few people actually do that, just like most don't fold their socks and underwear before putting them away. The important thing is to do *some* cleaning every time you fire any gun, especially if it's black powder.

Simply running a bore rod with a lube-soaked patch through the barrel once or twice removes the majority of gunk and is "good enough" for most post-use cleaning. <u>Remember to put the safety on when you finish.</u> Take the time to have someone experienced and knowledgeable show you how to clean your weapon the first time you do so, possibly the person who sells it to you, and don't be shy about asking for help if you need it. Please note that just as shooting with black powder is different from shooting a modern weapon, so is cleaning a black powder firearm.

At least once or twice a year, depending on how often and how much you shoot, take a few hours and do a thorough cleaning. Unless it's something you use year-round, this should be the last thing you do before storing it until next year. A few days beforehand, inventory your supplies and buy anything you may not have enough of. A bore rod, cleaning lube, solvent, bore cleaning brush, a patch holder, and cleaning patches are the most basic items you need. Depending on how thorough you are and whether you need to repair or replace any parts, you may need a vise and other specialty items. (If you are not an adult, make sure an adult is with you any time you handle a weapon until and unless your parents agree you are knowledgeable enough to do so without an adult and local laws also permit it.)

Now that you have supplies gathered and time set aside, clear a good size flat surface such as a table top to work on. If you can't find an area where the floor is a fairly smooth surface (wood, tile, linoleum), then put a sheet on the floor before you start work. Firearms have small pieces when you take them apart for cleaning and maintenance and it is far too easy to lose them in carpeting. Deeper cleaning involves taking your firearm partially (or even completely) apart to clean more pieces and then reassembling it. This makes it an ideal time to look for any worn or damaged pieces that may need repair or replacement.

How often you must do these things and how long it will take depends in part on the firearm and in part on use. Revolvers arguably need the least care, but even they do require it. A high-powered hunting rifle with a top-end scope will require more care in handling and in cleaning than just about any revolver in existence. It simply has more parts. A firearm that has had 1000 rounds go through it on many different days, in all kinds of conditions, including wet and muddy ones, will naturally require a lot more cleaning than one that has had 100 rounds go through it at an indoor range with no exposure to the elements. That's just common sense.

Storage

No firearm should ever be left unattended.

That is a laudable goal, but unrealistic. It would require every gun owner to carry every one of their firearms at all times, no matter where they are or what they are doing. That's where storage comes in. **Proper storage makes both accidents and theft much more difficult.**

Gun safes are the most common way to ensure other people can't shoot a firearm. Gun safes come in all sizes from tiny ones that can be bolted into a dresser drawer to full-scale rooms that resemble home armories. A safe bolted into a drawer won't prevent theft (they can take the drawer and get the gun out later) but it will still prevent accidents and make theft less likely by making it harder to find the gun. Even the simple lock on a concealed carry purse or a vehicle's glove compartment is a help.

Trigger locks are another option, but after looking online for information, they aren't one I can in good conscience recommend. They probably work for some firearms and in some instances, but clearly not for all of them. The article and video in the Resources section of this chapter do an ample job of explaining how a firearm can be shot even with a trigger guard installed.

Repairs

Find a gunsmith or someone who really knows what they are doing. A poorly repaired gun can be extremely dangerous. It is not child's play, or a game of any sort. A good gunsmith should also be able to help you learn how to properly clean and reassemble your firearm.

Concealed Carry

Most states have training and minimum age requirements for concealed carry permits and they vary by state. Having a concealed carry permit in one state does not guarantee you the right to legally carry in another state. That requires reciprocity, or a reciprocal agreement where both states agree to honor permits from each other. Reciprocity can change periodically, so check before traveling to another state unless you have looked recently.

When you have a firearm with you, it is either concealed carry or open carry. Open carry means people can see the firearm (open to view). Concealed carry means it is hidden (concealed from view). Most people who carry on a regular basis have a concealed carry permit and there is generally a minimum age requirement. There are a lot of options for carrying, most of which end up with them on your person in a holster of some sort. A few are in jackets, binders, purses, or other oft-carried items. If you carry that way, make sure to keep that item with you at all times. You can't leave your purse or jacket in a shopping cart or on a table while you turn your back "for a second" because it could be stolen that quickly, and you really, really don't want to be a person whose firearm was stolen.

Activity

Ask someone who lives with you to put a fake firearm (Nerf is fine, or a cap gun if you can find one) somewhere you are likely to encounter it within the next day but they can't tell you where. When you find it, follow the instructions for "what to do if you find a gun."

Quick Quiz

T/F   Ear and eye protection are completely optional when you are target shooting.

T/F   Only expensive ear and eye pro are effective.

T/F   It's important to do at least a quick cleaning every time you fire a firearm.

T/F   Concealed carry laws are the same in every state.

T/F   Everyone should have firearms safety training.

Resources

Articles

*Demo of Why You Should Wear Safety Glasses While Shooting
www.pagunblog.com/2007/04/23/demonstration-of-why-you-should-wear-safety-glasses-while-shooting/

*Easy and Effective Gun Maintenance
www.gameandfishmag.com/hunting/hunting_guns-shooting_gf_aa116902a/

Gun Cleaning Rules
www.otistec.com/support/gun_cleaning_rules.asp

Hunting Safety
homestudy.ihea.com/hsafety/index.htm

On Trigger Locks
www.donath.org/Rants/OnTriggerLocks/

Recreational Firearm Noise Exposure
www.asha.org/public/hearing/Recreational-Firearm-Noise-Exposure/

Other

Ear Buddy Ear Plugs 50 pairs
www.amazon.com/dp/B00PSX6ZV2/

Protective Shooting Glasses
www.amazon.com/dp/B000F7R47U/

Scouting-Specific

Rifle Shooting
meritbadge.org/wiki/index.php/Rifle_Shooting

Shotgun Shooting
meritbadge.org/wiki/index.php/Shotgun_Shooting

Videos

Complete Beginner's Guide to Gun Maintenance
www.youtube.com/watch?v=ITIQbM7xiSk

Never Use a Trigger Lock
www.youtube.com/watch?v=S_4QvNmfti4

Tree Stand Safety Course
www.huntercourse.com/treestandsafety/

ANSWER KEY

Chapter 1.	Chapter 5.	Chapter 9.
1. T	1. T	1. F
2. T	2. F	2. F
3. T	3. T	3. T
4. F	4. T	4. F
5. F	5. F	5. F

Chapter 2.	Chapter 6.	Chapter 10.
1. F	1. T	1. F
2. T	2. T	2. F
3. T	3. T	3. T
4. F	4. T	4. T
5. F	5. T	5. T

Chapter 3.	Chapter 7.	Chapter 11.
1. T	1. T	1. F
2. T	2. F	2. T
3. T	3. T	3. F
4. F	4. F	4. F
5. T	5. F	5. T

Chapter 4.	Chapter 8.	Chapter 12.
1. F	1. F	1. F
2. F	2. F	2. T
3. F	3. F	3. F
4. F	4. F	4. T
5. F	5. T	5. T

Chapter 13.

1. T
2. T
3. T
4. F
5. F

Chapter 14.

1. F
2. T
3. T
4. T
5. T

Chapter 15.

1. F
2. T
3. T
4. F
5. T

Chapter 16.

1. F
2. F
3. F
4. F
5. F

Chapter 17.

1. F
2. T
3. F
4. T
5. F

Chapter 18.

1. T
2. F
3. T
4. F
5. T

Chapter 19.

1. T
2. F
3. F
4. F
5. T

Chapter 20.

1. F
2. F
3. F
4. T
5. T

Chapter 21.

1. F
2. F
3. T
4. T
5. T

Chapter 22.

1. F
2. F
3. F
4. T
5. T

Chapter 23.

1. F
2. F
3. F
4. T
5. T

Chapter 24.

1. T
2. F
3. T
4. F
5. F

Chapter 25.

1. F

2. T

3. T

4. T

5. F

Chapter 26.

1. F

2. F

3. T

4. F

5. T

Acknowledgments

One of the challenges all writers face is getting a great cover. My thanks to Kim Hill for her help on the cover, but true credit goes to the photographer and the artist who created the original mural:
Carol M. Highsmith's America, Library of Congress, Prints and Photographs Division.
They are the source for the cover image, a photo of a beach mural by Sandy Rusnka (LOC #04178).

If you would like to support the work being done by Ms. Highsmith, artwork is available for purchase at:

photographs-america.hostedbywebstore.com/

Of course, if it wasn't for my own two crazy boys, I wouldn't have had the experience to know what I needed to write. So, my most sincere and deepest thanks to my two crazy boys, and my beloved and ever-supportive husband.

ABOUT THE AUTHOR

Bethanne Kim's mom took her to Brownies when she was six and she has been motivated to Be Prepared ever since. The importance of being prepared for emergencies hit home after she moved to Los Angeles. Earthquake preparedness is important there for obvious reasons. Since that was shortly after a boil-all-water alert in the city where she lived before that, and she worked in Florida shortly after a major hurricane wreaked havoc, she made sure her family earthquake kits (car, home, work, and school) were always up to date.

She left LA and moved back to the Eastern Megalopolis about the time the "prepper" movement really started. After years of hearing the importance of earthquake preparedness on top of years of Scouting's message of "Be Prepared", this message really hit home for Bethanne and she started following The Survival Mom's website. Shortly after that, she started writing for it.

Preppers are people who strive to be prepared for whatever hard times life throws at them by setting aside money, food, and other basic supplies so they have them in the event of an emergency. While this can include big, scary apocalyptic events like an EMP, mostly it means "everyday" emergencies like a blizzard taking out the power, hurricanes, the car breaking down on an isolated road, and job loss. (Job loss = no money for food, electricity, etc. – especially if you are unprepared.)

Another part of preparedness is knowing how to do things yourself, without calling in a specialist. Growing your own herbs and vegetables, and building the greenhouse to do that in, are perfect examples of this. Knowing basic first aid and simple home remedies (possibly uses herbs you grew in your garden) to reduce doctor trips is another.

Bethanne is writing this series of books to help others see that basic preparedness isn't rocket science. Our grandparents and great-grandparents had and used these skills, although it is easy to forget that.

Other Books by Bethanne Kim (Paperback)

The Constitution: It's the OS for the US explains the historical context for the US Constitution and describes how it works using computer terms like firewall and plug-ins, not legalese. (An OS is a computer Operating System, like iOS for Apple devices.)

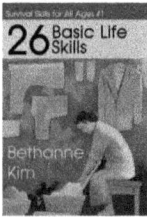

Survival Skills for All Ages Book 1: 26 Basic Life Skills covers skills so simple most emergency preparedness books skip right over them. In true emergencies, knowing how to sharpen kitchen knives and basic sanitation can be literal life savers. Skills were chosen for their value in everyday life and emergencies.

Survival Skills for All Ages Book 2: 26 Mental & Urban Life Skills covers financial skills, staying safe while traveling, self-defense, cyber security, hiding from danger, handling your emotions (including stress and anger), and more. These skills can help kids and adults throughout life, not just in emergencies.

Survival Skills for All Ages Book 3: Simple Cooking for Families is full of simple recipes that can be cooked using long-term storage ingredients and basic farm produce (fresh dairy and eggs), and recipes for staples such as mayonnaise, baking powder, sweetened condensed milk, and crackers. It also describes tools you can use to cook without power.

Survival Skills for All Ages Book 4: Simple Cooking for Allergies: Oral Allergy Syndrome and Low Histamine Food explains what foods are low histamine, why others are high histamine, and how to eat a low histamine diet while also avoiding the uncooked fruits and veggies that can cause problems for oral allergy syndrome sufferers.

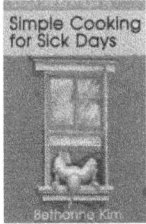

Survival Skills for All Ages Book 5: Simple Cooking for Sick Days is full of simple recipes that can be cooked quickly and easily, and that are easy to digest. When you or someone you care for is sick, it can be hard to think of palatable meals in the moment. This book includes both homemade meals and easy grocery store-purchase ways to make the same meals.

Cubmastering: Getting Started as Cubmaster is an introduction for new Cubmasters. Topics covered include organizational structure, training, recruiting, and recharter. This is about more than just the nuts and bolts of Scouting, though. It also covers dealing with difficult parents and planning special pack events.

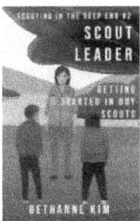

Scout Leader: An Introduction to Boy Scouts focuses on the nuts and bolts of the Boy Scouts of America with particular emphasis on how units in Cub Scouts and Scouts BSA are supposed to work. Recharter, training, common BSA meetings (such as Roundtable), and much more are described. Each chapter starts with a quote from Lord Baden Powell.

Citizenship in the World: Teaching the Merit Badge is, quite simply, a guide to assist merit badge counselors in teaching the BSA Eagle-required merit badge "Citizenship in the World." It includes the merit badge requirements, and information and tips for teaching it.

The Organized Wedding: Planning Everything from Your Engagement to Your Marriage is chock full of checklists. No detail is too small! What truly sets it apart is including the actual wedding ceremony and a chapter on your marriage with questions on financial priorities, family health history, and all your doctors.

OMG! Not the Zombies! Book 1 A group of teens goes for a hike and accidentally starts the zombie apocalypse. Being good at being prepared, they start setting up a safe community in the old Indian cliff houses and stocking it with supplies to save themselves and their families while the adults are still pretending life is normal.

BRB! Not the Zombies! Book 2 As their group grows, they discover a new mission: Get crucial information and items to the CDC to help with efforts to create a cure for the Infection. They fight their way through zombie-infested towns and to find the "impregnable" CDC research station their hopes are pinned on.

YOLO! Not the Zombies! Book 3 Have you ever wondered how a hurricane might affect the zombie apocalypse? Or how undead would fare in a sandstorm? (Hint: Hope they aren't wearing a helmet.) These and other natural disasters are explored in these zombie short stories.

Works in Progress:

Survival Skills for All Ages: 26 Outdoor Life Skills covers basic camping skills such as knot tying, fire building, outdoor cooking, and choosing a tent. It also covers hunting, fishing, and foraging for food; finding your way using maps, compasses, and GPSs; and truly basic skills such as managing time and water safety (tides, currents, etc.).

Survival Skills for All Ages: Special Needs Prepping may sound like something only "other people" need but the truth is that most families have special needs. Babies, elderly parents, diabetes, asthma, allergies–most of us have at least one of these and even if we don't, a simple sprained ankle or back injury can make us (temporarily) special needs.

Scouting in the Deep End: Association with Adults

CONTACT THE AUTHOR

Bethanne Kim would love to hear from you! You can connect with her through:

Email: bethanne@BethanneKim.com

Blogs: BethanneKim.com

Facebook: BethanneKim

Pinterest: BethanneKim

Twitter: @Bethanne_Kim

Because Amazon reviews really do matter, especially for indie authors, please take a few minutes and post a review of this book on Amazon.com.